SILENCE
SPEAKS

SILENCE SPEAKS

*from
the chalkboard
of
Baba Hari Dass*

SRI RAMA FOUNDATION

Santa Cruz, California
1977

© 1977 by Sri Rama Foundation, Incorporated

All rights reserved including the right of reproduction
in whole or in part in any form

Published by Sri Rama Foundation, Incorporated

Design and Illustration, Dharani Dass

Photography, William B. Giles

First Edition, January, 1977

Library of Congress Catalog Card Number 76-53902
ISBN 0-918100
Printed in the United States of America

BABA HARI DASS

CONTENTS

LIBERATION

In God's creation everything is possible. If one desires to be unattached he can be unattached, and if one wants to be attached he can be attached. The former will attain peace and the latter will attain pain. This is the only difference.

A person is in bondage by his own consciousness and he can be free by his own consciousness. It's only a matter of turning the angle of the mind.

When you are awake, the dream is gone. When you are enlightened, maya *is gone.*

What is the purpose of life? Why are we here?
To find God. To love God is man's natural state.

If you say it's natural, why do we have to work so hard to come to it?
There is the pull of the world. Stop the pull of the world and you will see that you are in God.

To search for enlightenment — is it like being ill? We search until we are cured?
We all are ill from illusion or ignorance. The world with desires is an illusion; without desires it is truth, love, God.

Is it possible for anyone here to get enlightenment in this lifetime?
The state is already there; it only needs to be awakened.

What happens in your navel when you get enlightenment?
A lotus pops out! (Joking)
Nothing happens in your physical body; it happens in the head.

Can we gain liberation through intellectual understanding of systems or theories?
There is no end to intellectual understanding. It doesn't give feeling, just as memorizing the definition of "liberation" won't give one liberation. The more we forget intellectual games, the more devotion we develop. In surrendering to God we don't have to read scriptures, we don't have to attend lectures of priests, saints, or psychologists. We just have to do it!

How do I find God?
Open your heart in front of God and He will listen to your prayer. A yogi searches for God in the world and says, "This is not God . . . this is not God . . . this is not God," and he

3

rejects everything. As soon as he finds God he says, "This is God . . . this is God . . . this is God." He begins to see God in everything and accepts everything.

What does it mean, "God is the Great Unmanifest?"
God is the creator of the world. We don't see His form. We don't know how He came into existence. His creation is He.

Is it possible to understand God without form?
It is easy to worship a form because we can see it and feel it. But God is beyond name and form. Our desire has created the form and we worship our desire. It's a good method, but after reaching a higher stage the name and form disappear. In worshipping God with form, one attains God according to one's own vision of Him. This illusion will take one to the true God. When I was a little boy I thought that God was like a giant who walked on the roof.

And now what do you think that God is like?
I don't think He has legs.

God is Magic.
God lives in the heart.
We can't see Him because our eyes
don't see inside ourselves.
But if you try to see inside yourself,
then you can see Him.
He is not air, but air is a part of Him.
He is not water, but water is a part of Him.
He is not earth, but earth is a part of Him.
Just like your nose is not you,
but it is a part of you.

Letter to a child

An aspirant attains the very God that he forms in his mind. If he thinks God is light, God appears as light. If he thinks God is sound, God appears as sound. If he thinks God has a human form, God appears in a human form. Actually, all these appearances of God are the illusions of the mind, because God is beyond name and form. He is everything and nothing. But the illusion is true to the person who sees it, and it brings a conviction of truth in him.

God is not somewhere else; you are God. You are God and you are in God. It's simply a matter of acceptance. Accept yourself, accept others, and accept the world. You will see everything is full of love, and love is God.

When a person starts loving God, he is not very far from Him.

A bird flies into a room and can't get out. She flies all over the room searching a way out, and when she can't find a way she gets tired and simply sits in one corner. Then someone opens the door and takes the bird out. We fly around in the room of the mind, and when we realize that there is no way to get out, we sit peacefully and wait for God to free us.

Pain will come, just like pleasure. Hate will come, just like love. And when both are accepted, unaffected by the mind, then there will be peace.

When the heart gets softer by being closer to God, one begins to feel love everywhere. Animals, trees, plants, people, and a blade of grass all shower love. It is a very good stage in Bhakti Yoga. I wish you deep, deep in love of God; I wish you to dissolve in God.

What is love . . . is it real?
Lover is a form, and love is beyond that form. Lover is body, and love is soul. Love is reality. That which is experienced by lovers is not love because it is mixed with attachment.

How can one develop real love, that which is above the physical plane?
To make the heart bloom, we have to stop hating others, as well as ourselves. Hate is like a frost which freezes the lake and burns the stem of the lotus flower.
Love is free from all bondage. It cannot be created by our minds, nor can it be made by our bodies. It exists in its own purity and shines by itself. A lotus blooming in a lake attracts the eyes of everyone, although it doesn't try to attract. When the lotus of love blooms in the lake of the heart, everyone can see it, feel it, and then they come like bees to take its nectar. When real love is understood, the heart will open like a lotus when the sun rises. Let love develop inside your heart. The purer the heart becomes, the more love will come out, and one day you and love will become one.

*God is the only lover and He loves in different forms —
parents, husband, wife, friend, children, animals. All are His
forms and He, Himself, has no form.*

**It is difficult for the average person to imagine a formless
God.**
*Accept God in all forms and no form, and be happy. God is a
mother, yet we must take care of our own needs. God has
arranged everything, but we must learn to accept it. It is
wrong thinking to expect God to come and put food in your
mouth. But if one has surrendered his ego totally, he is like
a small baby whose needs will be supplied.*

**How does one know that he is arriving at this surrender to
God, and not just using the concept as an excuse to not take
responsibility for his actions?**
*First comes contentment, then dispassion; one doesn't feel
anger, hate, jealousy, and so on. For him love is spreading
everywhere. When these qualities appear, that is called
surrender to God.*

*One who gets extreme desire for liberation becomes worthy
of liberation.*

9

The Self is like an ocean. Its real nature is very peaceful. The waves in the ocean are the universe, which is our own mind. The nature of waves is to go up and down. The waves are not other than the ocean; still we separate them by giving them a separate name and form. It's not unnatural for the mind to get stirred up by some external forces, but one who is aware of his own Self, "I am not the body and mind, I am pure Self," and knows that the universe is one with himself, will not be disturbed even though the waves are there.

*Self is God. But as long as we don't find God within ourselves
there is a difference between God's will and our will. We need
complete surrender to find God within ourselves. Complete
surrender doesn't mean not to work, not to eat, not to meet
people, but rather the ego of "I am the doer" should be
eliminated from the mind. What happens then? The mind
begins to accept all situations and becomes free from
pleasure and pain. It develops dispassion, and dispassion
brings enlightenment. In words the method seems very easy,
but it's a very difficult thing to surrender. It needs constant
practice and watching our every action. Without watching
ourselves we can't be aware of the tricks the mind plays. So a
yogi should be alert all the time.*

What is spiritual and what is material?
God and the world.

With what desire are we created? Why is the soul created?
The soul is not created by desires. It is like a shadow of God inside a being.

A gold piece covered by mud looks like a rock, but as soon as the mud covering is broken the gold piece shines and is clearly separate from the mud. This body, the senses and their creation, worldly illusions, are the covering on the Self — just like a thick cloud covers the sun. The Self is never really affected by the body and mind; they merely hide its glory. It is always separate, like a lotus leaf in the water.

MIND

What is mind?
A heap of thoughts.

What is an idea, a thought?
The idea is to attain peace.

How is the world created? The world is created by our own mind. By our own mind it is expanding; by our own mind its reality exists. Everyone's world is his own mind. Just as one can't dream anyone else's dream, so one can't see the world of others. But we all exist in the worlds of each other. Anything which is accepted by the mind comes into its existence, and when it is rejected by the mind its existence disappears. The world is just like a dream that is created by the mind and is experienced as real until the person awakens; then it disappears. The seer and the object seen make an illusionary relationship. If the seer loses his identity, the ego of being a seer, then the illusion doesn't exist in the object seen. There remains a reality — unchangeable, indestructible, immortal — which is God.

God is another name of truth. In search of truth a person searches the root of his existence. What is the root of existence? The root is ego, or we can say existence in the world is ego.

How do you define ego?
Ego is life. To keep the body's existence is ego. It is the part of the mind which identifies a creature with the world. Ego self tells you, "This is my body," and also tells you, "This is my Self." It connects the two. Without it a man couldn't understand the Self. Ego ends in the bliss sheath, Anandamoya Kosha. *Ego is the vehicle which can take you to this sheath and by which you can reach enlightenment.*

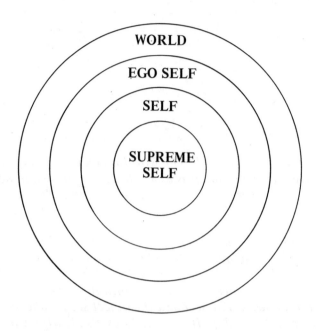

There are three kinds of Self:
  Supreme Self – God, the purest form,
  Self – the reflection of God inside the being,
  Ego self – identifies jiva *(being) with the world.*

And ego, itself, is qualified in three ways:
  On the Gross level there is tamasic ego: negativity, lust,
  anger, hate, jealousy, etc.; the mind is overpowered by
  its passions.

  On the Subtle level there is rajasic ego: a mixture of
  negative and positive qualities; the mind is filled with
  desires of power, and also compassion.

  On the Causal level there is sattvic ego: all positive
  qualities; the mind is filled with dispassion and desire to
  attain the truth.

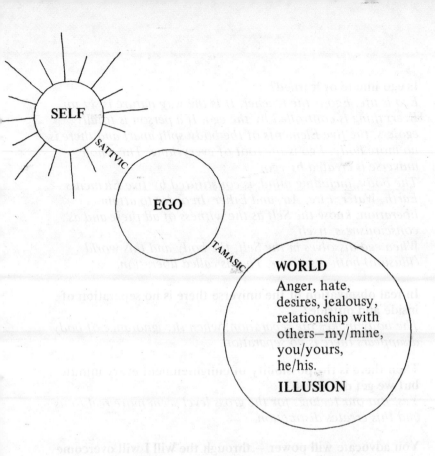

SELF

SATTVIC

EGO

TAMASIC

WORLD
Anger, hate,
desires, jealousy,
relationship with
others—my/mine,
you/yours,
he/his.
ILLUSION

*Ego can go in two directions: when the ego is channeled
towards Self it becomes sattvic ego, which is always good;
when it is channeled towards the world, it is called tamasic
ego, which makes illusion.*

*Ego is the bridge between the Subtle Body and the Self;
the Self can be felt by some part of the ego, otherwise we
wouldn't have any desire for God or liberation.*

*Ego cannot be stopped, only reversed. It can flow toward
the world or it can flow toward God.*

17

Is ego innate or learned?
Ego is life. Ego is the teacher. It is the way nature is set up. Everything is controlled by the ego. If a person is totally egoless, the five Elements of the body split apart and there is no more body. Ego is the root of everything. The whole universe is created by ego.

The body, including mind, is constituted by five Elements — Earth, Water, Fire, Air, and Ether. In order to attain liberation, know the Self as the witness of all these and as consciousness, itself.

When ego dissolves in the Self, the body and this world (illusion) both disappear. That is called liberation.

In real observation of the universe there is no separation of inside and outside?
The body makes the separation; when the ignorance of body disappears there is no separation.

Then there is the possibility of enlightenment every minute, but we get distracted?
Yes. But our feelings for the gross level seem more real to us and this creates distraction.

You advocate will power — through the will I will overcome this, etc. — isn't this more ego?
What is not ego?

As long as we are the doer, everything is ego. Development of positive ego power is will power. But ego is the only thing that keeps us alive in the world.

What is free will and its relationship to what appears to be free will?
You are free to grab a hot iron or jump from a cliff. You know it is dangerous. If you do it and say it is the will of God, that is wrong. God has given you a mind, but the mind is guided by some super power. So we have free will and we don't have free will — like a goat tied with a long rope. It

*can roam a good distance, but at some point it comes to the
end of the line.*

What is the difference between ego effort and divine will?
*By ego effort we reach the true Self. When ego self dissolves
into the true Self, everything becomes God's will.*

**It's hard to believe in God's will when the world is full of war
and famine.**
Belief in God's will is not for weak people.

How can one find peace in this world?
*As long as we have the ego of being a doer, we can't be
free. Diving for pearls is easy but when you have pearls you
develop fear of losing them. There is no peace; so diving for
God is better, although harder.*
*Peace, or freedom, can be attained by surrendering to God.
Do your* sadhana *(spiritual practice) regularly and offer it to
God. Don't do it to attain powers or knowledge. Do it as a
humble servant of God, without expecting a reward from the
Master. Do it as a woman who gathers flowers from the
garden to make a garland for her beloved, and puts it around
his neck when he comes. Her beloved's happiness is her
happiness.*

The ego of free will keeps the world going on and on.
Without it all actions would be stopped.
All our actions in the world, in the waking or in the dream
state, are controlled by the ego self. This ego self is like a
bridge which joins the jiva with the Self. Ego self identifies
the jiva with the true Self and also identifies jiva with the
world. The Self is beyond pleasure and pain. All frustration,
anxieties, pain, pleasure are in the control of the ego self. All
impressions of our actions in past births (samskaras) *are*
hidden in this ego self and are the cause of births and deaths.
The ego self also controls the intuitive flashes one gets in the
waking and dream states. The more ego self goes toward the
Self, the more intuitive knowledge becomes clear; the more
ego self goes toward the world, the more intuitive knowledge
gets hazy.
Attachment to the world (my house, my garden, my son)
and the ego that "I am the doer" (doctor, lawyer, minister,
yogi) chains up a human being so tightly that he doesn't
want to lose his attachment, even though he knows that
when he loses it he will attain eternal peace. He wants to
remain in the pain of "I am the doer."
Ego is important for achieving success in the world, but if
directed this way it can be a great obstacle in attaining real
peace. A person is a social being; he can't live without a
society. But to move in society he needs existence, or ego.
Under such conditions how can a person get peace? A person
can get peace if he learns to live among people unattached.
If he understands the world is unreal and only a projection of
his ego, if he acts in the world only as if performing his duty,
then there is peace everywhere for him.
The three worst traps for the ego are: desire for sensual
objects, desire for wealth, and desire for fame. Of these
three, fame is the hardest to overcome and the last
attachment to go.

Once Ramakrishna Paramahansa said, "A doll made of salt tried to fathom the ocean, but dissolved on the way."

There is no end. The more we go, the more we have to go. This is the ego if one says, "Look what hard austerities I am doing; what hard sadhana I am doing; how much love and compassion I have." In comparison to the endlessness of God, everything in a human being is not even one grain of sand on a vast beach.
The world consists of seven lokas *(universes). This physical universe is the lowest form. America is a dot in comparison to the lokas, your city is nowhere, and you do not exist. Now, where is your ego?*

Surrender of Ego . . . *a story*

*Mount Kailasha is the abode of Lord Shiva and his wife,
Parvati. Once Shiva and Parvati were sitting on the top of
Mount Kailasha enjoying the cool air and looking at the vast
plains where there were cities, towns, jungles, rivers. Parvati
said, "My Lord, look! Thousands of your devotees are singing
in temples, living in jungles, caves, or by the river banks
meditating on you. Why don't you give salvation to those
who are so devotional and loving?" Shiva said, "My dear, let
us go and see those devotees. Now I am ready to give them
salvation."*

*Shiva disguised himself as a saint and Parvati as his disciple.
They came down to the world and entered a town. They sat
in a secluded place, and if anyone came to the saint he would
tell the person his past and future. In no time the word*

spread all over the adjoining towns that a high saint with powers of prophecy had arrived. Flocks of people eager to know their futures began to collect. One day a group of devotees came. They were singing and dancing, and all were intoxicated with devotion. After chanting, one devotee, who appeared to be the leader of the group, came forward and bowed to the saint. Very meekly he said, "Guru Maharaj, will you tell me when I will get salvation? I meditate in the winter for two and one half hours, sitting in water up to my neck. During summer I meditate for two and one half hours surrounded by fires. When it rains I sit in the rain and meditate. I meditate every day for eight hours, and for several years I have been taking only a single meal of fruits and milk each day."

The saint looked at him with much surprise and said, "Oh, you are doing hard austerities! You are a very good yogi. You have much devotion." Hearing this the man felt very good and was excited to hear about his salvation. The saint continued, "If you go on doing your sadhana regularly, you can get salvation after three births." The devotee was shocked at hearing this. With bowed head he went back to his group saying, "Still three births!"

Another man spoke about his sadhana, and the saint told him it would be seven births. In this way everyone asked about getting salvation. The saint told one ten births, another fifteen, others twenty or thirty. Finally, when all were finished, a small, thin, ugly man who had been hiding behind the others came forward. He was shy and afraid but he dared to say, "Sir, I don't do any sadhana, but I love His creation, and I try not to hurt anyone by my actions, thoughts, or words. Can I get salvation?"

The saint looked at the little man and then scratched his head as if he were in some doubt. The man again bowed to the saint and nervously said, "Can I sir?" The saint then said, "Well, if you go on loving God in the same way, maybe after a thousand births you too will get salvation."

As soon as the man heard that he could eventually get salvation, he screamed with joy, "I can get salvation! I can get salvation!" And he began to dance in ecstasy. All of a sudden his body changed into a flame. At the same time the saint and his disciple also changed into flames. All three flames merged into one and disappeared.

Shiva and Parvati were again sitting on the top of Mount Kailasha. Parvati said, "My Lord, I am very confused. You told the leader, who does such hard austerities, that he would get salvation in three births. Then you told the ugly man that he would get salvation in a thousand births, but you gave it to him instantly." Shiva said, "No doubt the first devotee had much devotion and was doing austerities sincerely, but he still had an ego about his sadhana. He had not surrendered his ego yet, and three births appeared a very long time to him. The other man had so much faith that even a thousand births were very short for him. He completely surrendered to me. I did not give him salvation; it was his own faith in my words. His emotions increased so much that he could not keep the body any longer. His essence of life, the Self, took abode in me."

INTELLECT

The mind and senses are for examination, discrimination, and identification with the world. They are also the traps in life that keep a person in ignorance; but without the mind and senses, peace can't be attained. An average person sees immediate gain, sensual pleasure, and can't ever see beyond — where there is peace.

The body is like a chariot made of eight substances: blood, skin, flesh, fat, bones, marrow, semen, and aura. This chariot is pulled by two strong horses, mental energy and pranic energy, which are mutually dependent. Mental energy is fed by pranic energy; but without the mind, prana *(life force) could not reach its goal, which is attainment of God. Mental energy has four functions:* Manas, *Mind, the recording faculty which receives impressions gathered by the senses from the outside world;* Buddhi, *Intellect, the discriminative faculty which makes judgments and separates the real from the unreal;* Ahamkara, *Ego, the faculty of identification, both with the world of objects and with God;* Chit, *Memory, the generalized field of consciousness in which the other three mental faculties merge and work together. We can't ignore the mind in Yoga because it is the instrument by which higher consciousness is attained. Without it the methods become a mechanical process.*

What does Intellect (Buddhi) do that Mind (Manas) doesn't?
*Manas functions within the senses; the Intellect (Buddhi),
above the senses. The Mind functions in relation to objects
because objects are perceived by the senses. For example,
when you see an airplane has crashed, it is the Mind that
processes that fact, not the Intellect.*

**When we get to a higher level, beyond senses, we perceive
differently?**
*Then we perceive reality, which is quite different from the
world.*

**So past and future can be perceived outside of senses, outside
of time?**
Past, present, and future are perceptions on a gross level.

**How is the discriminative function altered when one attains
liberation?**
*The mind assumes its sattvic form and discrimination is on a
higher level. For instance, one doesn't see a person's color,
caste, or country on that level. Discrimination between real
and unreal is what counts.*

What is unreal?
The world.

Is there a point where there is no discrimination at all?
When complete truth is obtained, there is only God.

**We are always judging things — what is the difference
between judging and discrimination?**
*Do you judge, or compare, or discriminate? Judgment is the
action of comparison plus discrimination. This is all on the
worldly plane. Discrimination between reality and illusion is
a function of higher consciousness, which comes when a
person attains* Samadhi *(highest stage of Ashtanga Yoga,
superconsciousness). Then there is no question of judging.*

In regard to discrimination, I always feel guilty for not having done everything right.
You are speaking about worldly discrimination. For that a person needs a clear mind; and even then each person sees everything differently according to his own point of view.

When we make worldly choices, must we take our feelings into account?
Your choices will depend on how you see things, how you understand, and how you feel. We all see according to our desire. For example, a man was singing devotional songs to God as his beloved; another man passed by and thought he was singing to attract women.

But what does one do about the discrepancy between what he feels and what he understands?
If you really understand, your feelings will agree with your knowledge. If there is a discrepancy it means you don't know. Feeling comes after knowing.

How can I discriminate between imagination and intuition?
Only by a purified mind — otherwise you can't tell the difference between brass and gold. Intuition is developed by purity of the mind. If the mind is involved in worldly affairs this energy is dissipated. Intuitive knowledge comes by deep meditation. It is not guided by any desires. It is a flash of higher consciousness.

Is there such a thing as omniscience? Is there anyone who is all-knowing, all-seeing?
It is the stage of Parama Siddha *— one who can see the world as if it were an apple on his palm. If there were no such thing there wouldn't be a word for it.*

You're saying our imagination manifests as this world?
It manifests in one sense. If you think of Mount Everest it manifests in your mind.

Do you mean man imagines nothing, it all exists?
Your imagination is limited to this world.

Some schools say we become what our minds dwell upon.
Yes, it's true.
*An insect captures another insect and hypnotizes him by
making a sound. The captured insect is so frightened that he
thinks of his enemy all of the time. This thought of the
enemy gets so dense that he, himself, changes into the form
of that insect. A monk sings* "Aham Brahma," *I am God, all
the time, and his mind concentrates on it so deeply that he
begins to feel that he is God.*

*Everything in this world is personal, but we are connected by
projection. I am in your maya . . . you are in my maya. But
individually the maya is personal because we are the
projectors. I am not projecting your maya. Ego in its tamasic
state equals maya. You gave rock a name, rock never said,
"I am a rock." We try to give understanding to the illusion
by giving names.*

Is it the truth to say that everything is meaningless?
Your saying that is also meaningless. If you think *that way, it
is another thing — it is a method of dispassion. When maya is
gone there is truth. Maya is a veil over truth.*

When enlightened, do we see the veils?
*I cannot see your maya or world, as I cannot dream your
dreams.*

*Knowledge can't be taught. It is attained by sadhana. The
knowledge that can be explained by words is not real
knowledge. It is like explaining sweetness, which you can't
feel without tasting. If you taste sweetness, you don't need
words to understand it.*

29

If the universe is illusory what is the knowledge gained by scientific methods?
There are three kinds of knowledge: jnana, vijnana, *and* ajnana *Vijnana is scientific knowledge of the Elements, jnana is knowledge of the Subtle Elements, ajnana is ignorance. Scientific knowledge is real as far as it goes. It is not an illusion if we relate to the world as real; it is illusion if we relate to the world as a projection of our minds.*

What does that mean, "The world is a projection of the mind?"
We see what we want to see. If we don't want to see something, we don't see it. This "want" creates the form of the object outside. But there is an object minus the "want" of the seer which is reality. One who sees that reality is called an enlightened being.

How does one change intellectualizing into knowledge?
Intellectual knowledge is different in each kosha *(sheath). A child has intellectual knowledge, but it is different from that of a man. There is a similar difference between the intellectual knowledge of an ordinary man and a yogi. By Yoga you can change the intellectual knowledge of the Gross Body into the intellectual knowledge of the Subtle Body. So the first thing is to realize the Subtle Body by meditation. The only way is to concentrate and make the mind able to understand reality. From books you can understand only so far, like seeing a picture of a fire — you can understand it is fire, but it can't burn your hand. A picture of a lion can show you what a lion looks like, but you can't feel the reality of the lion. Real understanding comes by experiencing.*

Sages say that learning is of no use, so why do it?
Anything you learn by the senses and mind is ignorance. Real knowledge can only be obtained by higher consciousness.

Can intellect aid understanding?
It helps in the beginning but cannot give full enlightenment.
The mind is the main instrument to gain enlightenment, but
enlightenment is only reached when the mind stops.

How can we stop the mind?
Not by hitting it with a hammer. Stop the mind by the mind.

Your questions can't go beyond intellectual understanding,
and one who goes beyond intellectual understanding can't
question.

From letters . . .

You should not be afraid of your mind. It revolts in every person in the beginning of yoga practice. The mind is like a wild horse that doesn't want anyone to sit on its back. When one tries to tame it, it jumps more. If you don't tame it, it will not jump, but it will not be used for uplifting the consciousness. So taming is very important.
One should not put too much pressure on the mind in taming it. Try to understand the mind peacefully. Just like a horse trainer feeds and pats the horse, slowly, carefully, and peacefully you can tame the mind. Living in jungles, fasting, and doing hard austerities is also a way, but it is dangerous and creates much pain. You should choose a middle path. Don't let the mind be scattered and don't put too much pressure on it. You will see that slowly it will change.

Ninety percent of everyone's mind is in confusion. One doesn't see, taste, smell ninety percent of what he could experience. Everything happens in confusion by reflex action. Because we have done the same thing over and over again for several births, ninety percent of the action in our bodies is reflex action. When we understand this confusion and try to really hear, see, taste, we can feel the difference.

The world itself is a question and its answer is inside us. By study, reading, or travel we will get something, but we cannot know the whole answer. We can get this only by concentrating deeply inside. When the mind is free from thoughts a person can see what he really is. He can discriminate real from unreal. It's a good practice to listen to and follow the guidance of your heart. It increases will power. But sometimes, when the mind is covered by some attachment or emotion, it can create delusion.

It's good that you can see your mind going to other objects and forgetting Yoga and your aim. You can pull in your mind again when you are aware of it. The mind is made of subjects and objects, so it's the nature of the mind to jump like a monkey from one tree to another.

One who is pretending to sleep can't be awakened. You know your mental games. You know how you make yourself sad and miserable. There is no medicine or Mantra (syllable, word, or phrase repeated in meditation) for that except to kick yourself and stop pretending to sleep. To meditate for the purpose of getting high is not meditation; it's simply an emotion. If you meditate for peace, which is calming the thought waves of the mind, then you can attain some reality.

To control the mind is the most difficult job in the world. So it needs much practice. Go on doing regular sadhana. Once the mind is hooked it can't run away. The mind always revolts when it is disciplined or when its out-going vrittis *(thought waves) are blocked. That's why some* sadhus *(renunciates) do hard* tapas *(austerity). But if you understand its nature then gradually, in three to four years, it calms down.*

Mind seeks comfort. When a little hardship comes, your mind thinks of the old days when you were with your parents and without any responsibilities. But time always changes. You can't ever go back and be the same. The heaviest burden in life is to carry on with the responsibilities. Without this, one can't grow. You are afraid of getting nothing from your hard work. If you do your work as a duty and leave the result to God, then you will not be afraid, upset, and depressed.

Don't think that you are carrying the whole world. Make it easy. Make it play. Make it a prayer.

The mind makes so much trouble in meditation. Instead of fighting it, can I make it my friend and ask it to come along and enjoy the peace?
It's very difficult to control the mind. It is said, "A mustard seed can stay on a bull's horn more easily than the mind can stay on one object." It means it is very difficult, but not impossible.

When people see thoughts on a subtle plane, do these thoughts have form?
Thoughts are given form by the mind.

I see thoughts like spirals.
In you it's true; some feel thoughts like tangled barbed wire.

Do you ever think about how your answers may be misunderstood?
I don't think!

Virtue and vice, pleasure and pain, all are mental states that affect us only when we identify ourselves with the mind and think of ourselves as doers and enjoyers.

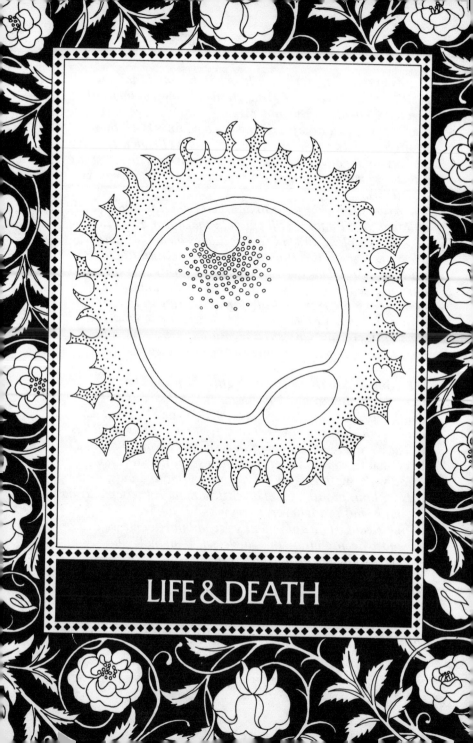

LIFE & DEATH

The essence of life in the world is absolute and omnipresent. Death is but a change of form. Human beings, animals, the vegetable kingdom, the mineral kingdom — all are alive. They take birth, grow, decay, and die (change form). All these forms are made by the mixture of Tattvas *(Elements), and all Tattvas are alive. Different kinds of forms with different kinds of qualities* (Gunas) *are created by the relative mixture of Tattvas.*

When one form changes into another form it is called death, although the life force still exists in that form. For example, as soon as a plant dies, a life force takes birth and starts to decay it. When it is completely decayed, a third life force starts working. This cycle of change of forms goes on and on, but the essence of life is always there — it is immortal. We measure the difference of life forces existing in various forms by our senses, but some life forces are beyond the capabilities of our senses. To measure these we must use instruments, such as the microscope or telescope.

When we see the tiniest animal made of a single cell, we see it is complete in itself. It eats, fights for possession, reproduces, and so on. This means it has the power of consciousness (mind), which is called Jnana Shakti; *it has action, which is called* Kriya Shakti; *it has matter, which is called* Karma Shakti. *These three Shaktis in one are called* Para Shakti, *which is God. In Hindu scriptures it is said, "God walks without legs, God works without hands, God eats without mouth . . ." This little animal is the same. It has no limbs, but it does everything without limbs.*

If our means of measurement were unlimited and we could see more deeply inside this single-celled animal, who knows . . . the whole universe is there.

One who takes birth will die. In other words, one takes birth to die. Death is sure and is always waiting. Because no one knows when one will die it is said, "Death comes from behind."

*Everyone has a fear of death. Everyone is attached to
ignorance. Everyone is afraid of salvation because no one
wants to leave this world. If God comes and says, "I'll give
you salvation if you are ready to die," you will see that not
even one percent will choose salvation. When you arrive at
a thoughtless stage in meditation your attachment to this
world comes in the form of fear and tells you, "Come back,
come back!" When Buddha was in deep meditation all such
things would come and disturb his concentration. The deeper
you go in concentration the more these ghosts come. But if
your aim is true these ghosts can't pull you down; you will
understand that there are no worldly pleasures.*

Is where we go in dreams similar to where we go at death?
*Life is also a dream, and death is the end of that dream. After
death another dream starts.*

Is it true that life is a preparation for death?
Yes, it's true.

Do we experience many spiritual deaths in a lifetime?
What is spiritual death?

Death of ego and attachment?
That is death of illusion, spirit doesn't die.

What can I do to overcome my fear of death?
*Attachment to the body causes fear of death. It is the
strongest attachment. Even a newborn infant has this
attachment. To overcome the fear of death it is necessary to
accept that we all have to die. No one can save us from death.
It is easy to say, "He will die," but we are afraid to face our
own death. Fear disappears gradually as bodily attachment
decreases.*

Is all spiritual work done on the physical plane, or on some other planes?
All three planes (Gross, Subtle and Causal) are together.

Why do we fear death?
Ignorance. Why are we afraid on a dark night? Because we can't see, and that is ignorance.

Some fear seems to be conditioned into us.
It has been developing from the day jiva (individual being) died the first time.

No one can change the world's cycle. A jiva will take birth, grow old, and die. But by developing faith one can be saved from fear of the future, fear of death. The jiva accepts that the responsibility is God's. One who identifies himself with the body dies because the body dies; one who identifies himself with the soul is immortal.

It's hard for me to work in an old people's home. It makes me feel terrible.
Why?

Everybody is dying.
So?

It's so unattractive.
It is also attractive. If you try to understand death, it can take away the fear of death. You can develop dispassion.

I feel repulsion.
If no one wanted to work with old people then what would happen to them?

I identify with their pain; that's what is so bad.
You identify with the fear of death. You don't want to accept that you also will go through the same process.

How can one help a dying person who has anger and fear?
It's very difficult for a person to accept death. He has fear, and fear creates anger . . . no fear, no anger.

Is that fear of bodily death or fear of the ego dying?
We relate death to the body. Body and ego are always together.

What is the fear of rebirth?
Rebirth means we have to die. There is no fear of rebirth, but fear of death.

The idea of going through this life again is dreadful!
That happens when a wife and husband fight. (Laughter)

Will Samadhi give complete understanding of death?
For a person who attains Samadhi, death becomes like replacing an old coat with a new one.

Your daughter was killed, and you know that she can't come again, and no one can bring her back. So the question should be erased from the mind.

The aim of life is to attain peace and bliss; in other words, that which is called God or truth. Now if you keep your mind busy thinking about the past events of family affairs, then you are sowing the seed of thoughts, which will make several branches, leaves, and fruits. You should know that freedom from thoughts is bliss, and that is called salvation. If you want to be in peace then cut the tree of family affairs which is growing inside your mind, and don't sow the seed of new thoughts. You are your own doctor. Forget the outer world and keep your mind free from past events and you will get salvation.

You wrote me about the death of your friend. Everybody takes birth to die. Every moment is reducing our age. Some are dead, some are dying, and some will die. No one will be saved from this death. The pitcher breaks but the air inside the pitcher doesn't break. The body dies, but not the Atman *(Self). He was your friend and he is still your friend. Forget his body and your attachment with his body. His Atman is alive.*

From letters

REBIRTH

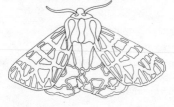

How do you interpret reincarnation?
*You mean rebirth? First understand what is death:
complete forgetfulness of past identities is death. When
memory is regained that is reincarnation, but when it is not
regained that is rebirth. In Hinduism there is no death; in
Christianity there is no rebirth. They are both the same . . .
the body never takes rebirth and Atman never dies.*

Remembering past lives, how does this happen?
*All actions are already in us from many births. Only an eighth
of our mind works, and the rest is in a dormant stage. When
the dormant mind is awakened one realizes all past lives, just
as if one saw them on T.V. By Yoga practice, or faith and
devotion, it can happen.*

So the process of remembering past lives is like untying a knot, and others who tell you about past lives don't know?
What is the proof? You must do it by yourself.

Is it important to know what your last incarnation was?
*It is important to eat the mangos and not to count the trees.
The important thing is to find out about the present birth;
then past will be known by itself.*

Are samskaras "original sin"?
*Samskaras are good and bad both. You may become
president by your samskaras, or you may become a thief.*

So good actions can bind us just as bad actions?
Any action binds. One binds with an iron chain, the other with a gold chain.

How can good actions be binding?
If you become president by good actions, still you are not free.

Is it attachment?
Yes.

Do we have control of destiny through God within us or through mind control?
Up to the limit of your mind you have control. If you touch fire it will burn. Don't blame destiny for it.

What is destiny?
Destiny is the result of samskaras, or tendencies, which are created by past karmic action.
Everything that has happened is within karma *(law of cause and effect). We can avoid certain karma by intelligence, but even intelligence is within karma.*

I get confused with karma.
It is confusing.

Could karma be defined as cause and effect?
Karma is action. It is cause and effect. There is no uncaused action nor is there any action without effect.

What constitutes non-karmic activity?
Non-karmic activity occurs when a person surrenders totally the ego of being a doer. The heart beats and the mind acts, so one is still active; to ignore this "I-ness" is still work. You are not the body. *When this becomes clear to you, then you will work and, at the same time, not work. Your body will function by reflex action.*

What is the difference between karma and samskaras?
Roughly we can say that samskaras are the impressions in the mind from earlier actions, or "conditioning." According to the theory of rebirth, one still carries the prints of actions from earlier births. They exist in layer upon layer. These layers can be peeled off by meditation or spiritual life. Samadhi is the one way by which these samskaras can be wiped out completely, and this leads to liberation.
Each lifetime is to live out the samskaras created in the previous lifetime. At the same time, your actions in this life are creating new samskaras.

Are there spirits from other realms who can give truth through a medium?
I only believe in Self. One who believes in ghosts is afraid of ghosts. If you don't believe, there is no fear. It is your emotion.

How does one explain the psychic abilities of some people, like Uri Geller? I've been able to do absent diagnoses.
Some are born with that talent, just as poets, musicians, painters, scientists are born with their talents. Some develop powers through Yoga methods by regular practice.

That should not be our goal?
In animals there are such powers by nature. A human being has all animal powers. They are in everyone. All we have to do is open up to what is already in us. But attaining powers and attaining the truth are two different things. If truth is realized, then there is no need of any powers.

When a saint exists in two different places at the same time, does he experience simultaneity?
Both forms can function differently. The awareness can be the same.

If one body was here and one body in Mexico, would only one of the bodies remember?
Both bodies will remember each other. They are not two, but two puppets controlled by one puppeteer — two bodies, one consciousness.

It seems that realization of the truth behind powers can enlighten the mind.
Enlightenment and realization of the truth are the same. A person who has powers can remain unenlightened.

What happens if enlightenment is not attained and samskaras not removed in this life?
You will begin in the next life where you end in this one. You cannot lose if you try.

Is everyone reborn and do they get a second chance if enlightenment is not attained? What if they don't believe in rebirth?
Rebirth is caused by the confused mind. If one had no desires then he wouldn't be reborn. A person dies in confusion, takes birth in confusion, and as long as he lives develops confusion. This illusion keeps him from knowing who he was, who he is, and who he will be. But when this confusion becomes less dense he begins to understand who he was and who he is. Yoga sadhana is the only way to get out of this confusion. It's most important to be aware of our actions all of the time.

How do we eliminate the effect of past deeds?
The effects of past deeds are called samskaras. They are eliminated in two ways: by attaining Samadhi, and by cultivating good qualities — contentment, compassion, tolerance, and so on.

By striving for and attaining these qualities, do we gain enlightenment?
Attaining enlightenment and wiping out samskaras are the same thing. As soon as the veil is taken away you are there.

46

As I understand it, karma continues from one life to the next. What then is the role of experiencing the karma of a past life during meditation?
How can you say it's not your imagination? You can't know of past incarnations until you attain higher Samadhi.

The higher you get, the better your memory gets, but also you supposedly get more dispassion. What's the purpose of the memory?
As consciousness gets higher, samskaras get thinner and one can see the past. It's consciousness, not the memory, that gets higher; the memory is incidental.

Does meditation affect the influence the planets have on us?
When meditation can change all threefold karma, it will have an effect.

Is enlightenment free from planetary effect?
What is enlightenment?

Getting rid of earthly limitations?
Realization of the truth is enlightenment, and truth has no limitations.

What is threefold karma?
It is: 1) Samchit *(collected), the unfinished mass of actions of past births, both good and bad, yet to be worked out and which appear in this birth in the form of desires — in other words samskaras; 2)* Prarabdha *(detained), the result of karma already worked out in a previous life which appears in the present life in the form of fate; 3)* Agami *(present), the karma we are continually making in our present actions and will be making in our future actions.*

How do we get rid of karma of the future?
When present and past karmas are conquered, there will be no future. Good actions wipe out past karmas and then

*future karma will automatically be good because there will
remain no bad tendencies to pull you to bad actions.*

How can I come to realize what is said about reincarnation?
It's not part of my experience.
*Without getting Samadhi, you can't experience it. Without
silencing the mind, you can't get Samadhi.*

Is it the ego that is reincarnated?
*Ego makes desire; desire makes rebirth. We are reborn to
fulfill our desires; and in fulfilling them, we make more
samskaras.*

Do we release samskaras through knowledge of past lives?
*Knowledge of past lives can show you the root and you can
dig it out, but knowledge of past lives is not easy to attain.
Some are born with the ability to know, but they are only
one in a million. This ability is lost by indulging in the world.
For others, attaining Samadhi gives knowledge of past lives.*

Are past lives important — to know about them, I mean?
*Past lives always count, but no one can prove past lives to
other people. Only by ourselves can we learn that the past,
present, and future are all one. An honest seeker of the truth
doesn't waste his time in trying to understand theories of
karma and samskaras, but accepts them and tries hard to
change them. The shore is not far for those who do not stop
swimming.*

Is it possible to reach a stage where you are no longer
creating karma? If you do your actions for your 'guru'
(teacher), do you get karma?
What kind of actions?

Helping others; doing what your guru has told you to do.
*Then you are collecting good karma. It is quite clear if you
do good, you get good. But you should be aware that helping*

*the poor or unfortunate is good for your samskaras; you
can't change the samskaras of others.*

Does the guru take on the disciple's karma?
*Can you eat for your baby? One who is waiting for his guru
to take his karma will remain sitting. One should take full
responsibility for his karmas and work on them.*

When one is enlightened is there still karma?
*Yes, the existence of such a being is karma; but one's actions
in this stage don't make imprints for a future life.*

Do you believe in Christ's coming in the second millenium?
*Higher beings come from time to time. The name and form is
not important.*

Do higher beings come with a purpose?
Their appearance itself is a purpose.

Is Christ going to come again in the body?
*He can come again at anytime. He doesn't need any special
body. Any body can become Christ.*

Can we work out our own samskaras, or do we need the help of someone else?
*You have to work out your samskaras by yourself. Help
comes by itself from time to time.*

How can we keep from forming more samskaras in daily living?
*Work in the world like a bank manager who works all day
with money but doesn't own it. He won't cry if the money is
stolen, but the proprietor will. If you can keep yourself
unattached from the action then you can't make bad
samskaras.*

It seems the game gets subtler.
The ego also gets higher according to your higher stage. The ego can even trap you by being kind, generous, honest. For that we must be aware at all times.

To transcend the ego seems hopeless.
Watching the ego becomes a habit; you have to become as alert as a thief. You can stop an action if you really think it's not good.

That's another judgement — "good."
You don't grab a burning coal! We are trapped again and again because we can't really discriminate between good and bad. We always discriminate according to our desire.

If it's desire that makes rebirth, can't we just desire not to be reborn?
What is the strength of that desire? A dog can be a human being if he desires it enough. But you know, a well-fed dog, if let loose, still digs in the garbage pile.

Is this an endless process, or is rebirth ever over?
There are several cycles. You shoot up from one to another.

But you remain an entity, just larger and more aware?
(Nods) This cycle never ends. Some day you can be a planet and again make circles around the sun.

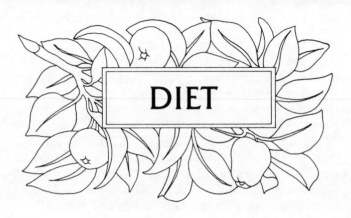

DIET

For sadhana a strong body and mind are required, so one
should eat good food. If the body is strong one can sustain
heat, cold, wind, rain, anything.

Don't make too many rules about food, just eat a simple,
pure diet, and forget about it. For Yoga sadhana a balanced
diet is best: vegetables, grains, fruits, nuts, and milk. We
don't want food that is tamasic (meat, fish, decayed or stale
foods), as this disturbs the Chit. We eat mainly rajasic (energy
creating) and sattvic (pure) foods. Milk is life — it is the first
food given by God, and so it is classified as sattvic. It causes
mucous, but mucous balances the burning quality of bile. A
diet too high in mucous, however, creates laziness, sex
desires, and overeating. Mucous is a very important part of
the body; in this season bile increases to keep the body
warm, strengthen the digestion and make a padding of
fat. Mucous type foods prevent the increased bile from
burning the stomach and intestines. For cold countries fat
producing food is important. During summer, when it is hot,
one can live on a fruit diet.

Is physical sadhana affected by diet?
According to Ayurveda *(classical Indian medicine), human beings are classified into three categories or Humors: Air predominant, Bile predominant, and Mucous predominant. Food is also classified in this way. The food we eat works differently for the different body types because of these three Humors. If one is Air predominant he must take food that reduces air (gas). Suppose a person has a weak Earth Element — grains, which are predominantly Earth Element and mucous producing, will help him. The idea is to maintain an equilibrium of the three Humors. All the five Elements exist in our bodies in a certain ratio; when the normal measure of any of these Elements is increased or decreased, the result is sickness. Yoga sadhana is also classified according to heating, cooling, and moderate methods. If a person is Mucous predominant (cool), he will need heating methods. So sadhana and diet are both related to a person's body Humor. If all three are perfectly in tune he will feel wonderful and sadhana will go very well.*

Where does sugar and a craving for it fit in?
Sweets are Mucous predominant and they decrease Bile and Air Humors. If a person craves them, his body is out of balance. However, when one begins doing Pranayama *(breath control), his bile increases; then the body needs more sweets.*

What are bile foods that aren't meat?
Eggplant, fruits, green leafy vegetables, yogurt.

How do the three Gunas relate to the five Elements, and the three Humors?
Tamas Guna is related to Earth and Water Elements and Mucous Humor; Rajas Guna, to Fire Element and Bile Humor; Sattva Guna to Ether and Air Elements and Air Humor. In this way everything is classified by the three Gunas; for instance, fruits have all three Humors (pulp, seeds, and skin). All herbs are classified like this too.

Is coldness Mucous predominant?

Mucous in itself is cold. Mucous predominant people can stand more cold.

What is the role of diet in consciousness?

If the diet is easy to digest and doesn't create too much heat or cold, it is good for the mind and body.

Is there a certain diet for Pranayama?

Wheat, rice, good corn, milk, ghee (clarified butter), sugar, dried ginger, garbanzo, cucumbers, figs, roots, fruits, eggplant, etc. Pranayama is very heating. When one does a lot of it he should eat cooling foods.

Does doing Yoga cause food to be assimilated more easily?

It enables the body to extract more from the food taken in.

Is it possible to live with no food?

It's not impossible; some sadhus do it.

What about a nun in Europe who took no water?

There was one woman saint in India also who lived without food. It's possible to develop the ability to extract life force from the air. In Samadhi, sadhus do not eat for thirty to forty days and still they remain healthy.

How often and how long should one fast?

Once a week rests the digestive system (from after dinner one night until dinner the next night). Medicine is needed according to the sickness; if you don't need fasting, don't do it for long periods. If the body is really impure, then do a three to nine day fast with hot lemon water to drink. There are several methods.

It's a good practice to go on a fruit diet for a week or a month, or to go on a liquid diet. It helps very much in purifying the body.

53

Why don't yogis eat meat?
Some do; if they live in Tibet, they have to eat meat to survive. But we get meat by killing. Is killing good? If we can live without killing it is better to do so.

Does the violence of killing pass into you when you eat meat?
The animal doesn't want to be killed. In eating meat you eat the animal's attachment to its body which remains in the meat.

My teacher eats meat; would you ever eat meat?
If it grows on trees. (Laughter)

It's been proven that plants have feelings too. Isn't it just as bad to eat them?
When you break a green plant it feels pain, but when it gets ripe it needs to be replaced. The same with fruit and flowers. Vegetable consciousness is different from animal consciousness.

I never felt I had interest in food until I decided to improve my diet. Now I think about food all the time!
Eat food and don't think about it.

I work around food and find myself eating all day long. How can I change?
Put a limit on your eating — two meals a day. A person can develop the eating habits of a goat! Mind makes the habit, mind can break it.

I know I'm attached to the body, but I try all sorts of diets. I don't know whether I'm Mucous predominant, or what I am. I don't know what to eat!
Eat what you can digest. If you think on food very much it also becomes a trap. Some people eat raw food. Raw food is good, but if you can't digest it, then it is bad for you. It can't be classified as a sattvic diet for you.

Is it best to eat just two meals a day?
Yes.

What is the best time space between meals?
Eat before noon and after sunset, approximately eight hours between meals.

One shouldn't eat between meals? I've heard that it's best to eat small amounts continually.
For what purpose? For Yoga, or for building the body? If it's for health it's all right. Eat like a goat . . . all day long. (Laughter) But for Yoga, if you eat two meals then your digestive system will work just twice and you can get enough time for Sadhana.

What spices can be used in a sattvic diet?
Spices are used in such a way as to balance each other. For example, turmeric with coriander, cinnamon with nutmeg, black pepper with anise seed. Garlic, onions, and hing (asafaoetida) are strong and hard to digest. Although garlic heals wounds and strengthens lungs, it is heating and not good for meditation.

Isn't it better to avoid all spices?
Spices are not very important. If a person is healthy he can digest anything.

What are the effects on the body of ginger root and cayenne? Some think they are a kind of "speed."
They are Bile predominant and heating. Ginger root reduces mucous, but long usage will dry up the system. Cayenne is a blood purifier and good for the eyes.

How about ginseng?
It's a Chinese herb, Bile predominant. I've experienced that it is good for the nerves and heart.

55

Do you in your own diet try to avoid chemicals, additives, pesticides, etc.?
I don't know about those things. I eat what I get. Don't make eating complicated. A sattvic diet is balanced and consists of food you can easily digest. Rules are made only when food is plentiful; in times of famine one eats what he can get.

The effects of Yoga practices are a strong appetite, good digestion, cheerfulness, courage, enthusiasm, a beautiful body, and strength. So why worry about food?

HEALING

Is there a system of healing or medicine which is superior?
*In each culture they have their own methods, and people
have faith in these. Mantra can cure a cobra bite if faith in
the Mantra is strong enough.*

*Faith is the most important thing in healing; still there are
medicines in every culture, it's part of nature. If God allowed
the creation of disease, He also allowed man to have the idea
of medicine. This is the natural balance. Even animals have
some idea of medicine; dogs and cats eat grass when they are
sick. I don't see why one should not go to a doctor or take
medicine if he is sick. Both Ramakrishna and Ramana
Maharshi suffered from cancer. They took medicines, but it
didn't mean that they were afraid of pain or death. If you
think there is something wrong with you, you should be
checked by a doctor. If you have a disease, it can be cured. If
there is no disease, then the fear inside of your mind will go
away, and automatically you will become stronger.*

Once Ramakrishna Paramahansa said, "Why cross a river by using siddhis *(extraordinary powers) when we can cross it by paying one cent to a boatman?" If a sickness is God's wish, then taking medicine is also God's wish. But nature cures the sickness of those who have complete faith in her.*

The body is not only for enjoying the world, we need the body as an instrument to worship God. If this is our aim, then we should try to keep the body fit. The Gross Body is the main instrument for doing sadhana. If it is well then sadhana goes well. The body is a chariot of ten wheels; if one wheel doesn't work then the chariot must slow down. Five Jnanendriya — *organs of experience (nose, tongue, eyes, skin, ears) plus five* Karmendriya — *organs of action (anus, genitals, legs, hands, voice) are those wheels.*

I know a doctor who has a fifteen year old son who has certain psychic powers, like Uri Geller. They are sincere people and they wonder if those powers could be used to heal people.
The boy has the state of Bhava Pratyaya, *which means born with powers, as some are born musicians or poets.*

Can he turn it into something useful, for healing?
The healer is purity of mind. If mind is pure, one can heal sicknesses. In healing there are three methods: Tantra, *which works by exciting the emotions;* Mantra, *which works through the chanting of sacred words or sounds; and* Yantra, *which works through geometric forms, colors, diagrams, as well as herbs and medicines.*

Why do so few yogis demonstrate the healing powers they supposedly have?
It's not good to have an abscess on the body. If they show their powers, people will follow them all the time. For a yogi, name, fame, and money are abscesses. Yogis accept God's program. If they get sick they will take medicine, but if they are dying they will not worry about it.

In healing doesn't one interfere with the cosmic plan?
Yes.

Does one pray and ask God if He wants to help?
Either take the sickness, or pray to God to relieve you of the samskara.

How does healing interfere with the cosmic plan? Isn't that interference also a part of the plan?
Yes, it just extends the time factor.

What about Christ's healing miracles, weren't they real?
Yes, they were real, but still all of those people died.

Why are some born with physical or mental handicaps?
There are many reasons: unhealthy environment, hereditary diseases, or sometimes bad samskaras — even good samskaras. Sometimes a saint needs just one more birth to finish all his samskaras. He might take that birth in a handicapped body. In this way he does not make more samskaras.

How does one discriminate when he is being kept alive by machines? Doesn't this interfere too much with the cosmic plan?
He will die anyway. Lock him up anywhere, and you still can't save him. It is scientific ego at work.

Do you feel pain?
If I say no, you'll hit me with a rock! I feel pain (then showed hip and finger which were injured in a game). It's a body function; all feelings are there, but the difference is how attached we are to pain.

SLEEP

Are there any rules for sleeping, is one position better than another?
The best position is on the left side with the right knee pulled up. This keeps the right nostril clear, which helps to keep the body warm. (Pingala, the heating breath, flows through the right nostril).

Can you comment on how much sleep people need? I find that five hours are not enough.
From age thirteen to twenty, eight hours; after twenty, six hours are enough. Sleep from 10:00 p.m. to 4:00 a.m.

I try to do that but sometimes I'm too excited to go to sleep at 10:00.
Still, wake up at 4:00. Gradually it will become a habit.

Regardless of what time I go to bed?
If you don't sleep one night, the next night you don't need twelve hours of sleep. The night after a sleepless night the sleep gets thicker, denser.

Is it true that more than six hours creates lethargy?
It depends on the food you eat and your digestion. If your digestion is good, you need only four hours.

What determines good digestion?
When food is well digested, then you don't need much sleep. Your body will be active and full of energy.

Does standing on the head help digestion? If so, when should it be done?
It helps. Do it after Asanas, or after meditation, but not after taking food.

How long should one stand on his head?
Up to five minutes and gradually the time can be increased to twenty minutes.

How much sleep do you get?
I don't get much sleep.

Why do we sleep so much?
Habit is difficult to break. You are taught to sleep more. Once you develop the habit of less sleep, it will not be difficult. But it needs practice. Take light food at night. The sheep herders in the Himalayas walk all night and sleep very little in the morning. It is natural to them.

Hallucinatory drugs are not good for Yoga sadhana. To get out of illusion one needs a pure mind free from all delusion. If one takes a drug and makes more delusions, then how can he get out of illusion? According to Ayurveda, ganja *(marijuana) is classified among the mind sharpening herbs, but it is used as a medicine. If it is used in bigger doses for a long time it can cause loss of memory and impotence. I knew*

several siddhas *(highly advanced yogis) who used it, but they were not householders; they had no responsibilities. It becomes addicting after some time and addiction of anything is a trap.*

Can we reach the same level of awareness alone, as with ganja and other drugs?
By Yoga you can attain much higher levels. Drugs merely excite the energy centers (chakras) *and can give you a glimpse of what it looks like.*

It's a general feeling among older people that all those who are in Yoga are drug people. It's a wrong idea. Drugs and Yoga can't go together. No one sits on the dirt while he is wearing clean pants.

How about LSD? It has given spiritual insight to many Westerners.
I don't think LSD is good for sadhana. It accelerates the change of Elements inside the body a hundred times more than usual, which causes visions of different kinds of geometrical patterns and different kinds of colors, light, and so on. LSD can harm any nerve in the brain permanently.

Do you recommend that we don't smoke ganja, if so why?
Ganja is an addiction, just like tobacco and other drugs. All addictions are harmful.

Why do sadhus smoke it in India?
The reason is that they don't want to face the world; they don't have to. They try to finish sexual desire by using ganja and turning their minds away from it.

But sometimes it is sexually stimulating.
In the beginning it is, but its regular use for several years causes impotence.

A lot of my friends and I smoke it regularly, it's a social thing. Everyone I know smokes ganja.
So . . . ?

What are the patterns of movement I sometimes see?
They are caused by the circulation of Elements — Earth, Water, Fire, Air, and Ether. Each hour the Elements make a full circuit, each one predominant for differing lengths of time. Each Element has a colored geometric form which can be seen. Earth is characterized by a yellow square; Water by a white crescent; Fire by a red triangle; Air by a blue star; Ether by a white circle. When these change, patterns are created and they make designs. LSD causes the patterns to change faster than normal. When one takes LSD he sees the patterns, but can't fix upon one Element. Concentration cannot be maintained and so one doesn't get the power of the patterns he sees.

Can't drugs be helpful in acquiring knowledge of the Self?
Then all here would be enlightened! (Laughter)

Once you said that smoking ganja enables one to talk to walls, could you clarify that?
Have you seen two people stoned on ganja?

Yes.
Did they say, "The lamp post is my brother?"

No.
Then not enough ganja. (Laughter)

Are there harmful effects from mixing ganja and Pranayama?
It is ganja Pranayama! It brings craziness. Ganja and Pranayama can't go together. Pranayamas are for increasing pranic energy. If smoke goes in, it will harm pranic energy.

Is there any truth to the theory that drugs make holes in the aura and reverse the polarity of the body?
No holes. I don't know about the polarity theory. I know very simple things.

Friends of mine used to sniff glue and they said that it makes the ears ring very loudly. Was that 'Nada' (Subtle sound)?
Nada means any sound, but Yoga is concerned with the Nada which appears due to purified nerve channels. The kind of intoxication you mention pollutes nerves. These impure nerves get excited, vibrate, and make sounds. It's not helpful to listen to that kind of sound.

I've heard that one can hear his electrical nervous system during meditation. Is that Nada?
Yes, in meditation movement of prana (vital energy) gets very clear. It also happens when one is in a high emotional state. One should be very still and concentrate. Nada intoxicates if one concentrates deeply on it.

What do you mean by intoxication? Is there then a good and a bad intoxication?
When the mind is intoxicated by Nada it feels very light, peaceful, and it doesn't want to indulge in worldly things. This state is also called dispassion.

How can there be a good and a bad intoxication?
One intoxication brings knowledge and the other brings depression. Swooning the mind by Nada and swooning the mind by a hammer are two different things. The swooning stage is the same, but the results are different.

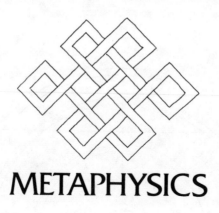

METAPHYSICS

*Nature is a force both inside and outside of us which governs
everything. Nature equals the three Gunas — Sattva, Rajas,
and Tamas. Sattva is purity, balance. Rajas is creative energy,
action. Tamas is inertia, resistance, and destruction. The
source of the three Gunas is Brahman (God), so everything
is controlled by God. In the beginning there is only pure
consciousness, which is represented by Sattva Guna. When
Rajas Guna (creative energy) and Tamas Guna (destructive
energy) overpower this pure consciousness, Sattva Guna
changes into maya, the universe. Then, in another burst of
energy, Rajas and Tamas again overpower Sattva, and avidya,
a state of ignorance, is created. Avidya is made of the three
Gunas in this way: Sattva Guna gives rise to the Subtle
senses, Rajas Guna creates the organs of action, and Tamas
Guna produces the five Elements (Earth, Water, Fire, Air,
and Ether). In this manner the three bodies — Causal, Subtle,
and Gross — are formed.*

Pleasure and pain occur when ignorance, Tamas Guna, is predominant.

Happiness occurs when creative energy, Rajas Guna, is predominant.

Bliss occurs when pure consciousness, Sattva Guna, is predominant.

No one can remain in the same mood all of the time. Within every hour the predominance of each of the five Elements changes in the body, and according to the predominant Element, the emotions and vrittis also change. Every two hours the predominance of the Gunas changes. Because of the continuing flux of the Elements and the Gunas, a person can't be established in one emotion for a long time.

In the beginning there was God in the form of sound. That sound is AUM, represented by the symbol ॐ *This symbol is composed of three Sanskrit letters (A) (U) (M), which stand for the three Gunas: (A) represents Rajas — creative, active energy; (U) represents Sattva — pure, balanced energy; and (M) represents Tamas — reactive, resistant energy. In Hinduism these energies are identified with three aspects of God:* Brahma, *the creator;* Vishnu, *the preserver, and* Shiva, *the destroyer. Thus AUM,* ॐ *is the sound of God, the sound of creation, and the sound of liberation.*

Before evolution begins, the Gunas are in a state of equilibrium in Mula Prakriti, *the seed center of* Sahasrara Chakra *at the top of the head. Mula Prakriti is unmanifested and eternal, yet it is the uncaused cause of the entire manifest universe. It is the inherent energy of* Purusha *(Self) and is inseparable from it.*

What is 'Kundalini?'
Kundalini is the energy left over from creation. It is stored at the base of the spine. When a person relaxes his body completely, his thought waves become very shallow. At that moment Kundalini energy, which is also sexual energy in its gross form, gets excitement and starts to move up. This stage makes a kind of pleasure that turns to happiness and then bliss in its later stages.

I've heard Kundalini is dangerous, that it can kill us.
Its real name is Kula Kundalini. *Kula means body, Kundalini means winding. What is winding the body? Anger, hate, jealousy, all bad habits. When those negative qualities are reduced, the awakening of Kundalini begins. When negative qualities are completely wiped out, liberation is achieved. In the physical body, there is a storehouse of energy at the base of the spine. This energy can be excited by Yoga, dreams, accidents, drugs, shock, sometimes by illness. If this energy is excited and a person is not able to handle it, he can be trapped in worldly desires.*

If one can awaken Kundalini by drugs, why do Yoga? Wouldn't drugs be faster?
If a person takes a drug he can be trapped — energy goes up and comes down hard. If one really tries to get energy excited, he can do it, but the method should be right. Only by Sadhana can one move the energy up with permanent benefits.

Is awakening of Kundalini necessary for enlightenment?
Yes. Kula Kundalini is made of six vikaras, *impediments — existence, birth, growth, change, decay, destruction — which bind the body. When this chain is broken it is called awakening of Kundalini. When some symptoms appear in the physical body, like the appearance of light, sound, sensations, we say that Kundalini is awakening.*

Is it possible for the Kundalini to go up and down?
Yes. It goes up and down until it pierces Ajna Chakra *(between the eyebrows) and the first stage of Samadhi is attained. Then it stays more stable. You can get all knowledge after piercing Ajna.*

In terms of macrocosm-microcosm, the sun is called the source of Kundalini?
It is known as Atman. In our body Kundalini is the sun.

What is the difference between a person and a star?
Man is complete in himself, so he himself is one star. Nothing goes outside of the psyche — this is the beauty of God. Everyone is so perfect.

If all is one, what is bad?
We don't see all as one, and that is bad.

I was reading in Sri Iso Upanishad **that this universe is finite like a coconut; beyond that is the spiritual sky.**
There are seven sheaths to the universe. Everything we see — stars, planets, earth — are within the first sheath.

What is beyond the seventh sheath?
It's called Loka Lok, *or* Shunya, *or God.*

Could a spacecraft get to Loka Lok?
If it doesn't dissolve.

Into different substances?
Different temperatures, forces of gravity, gases. But we have not yet even fully discovered the human body.

Is Loka Lok inside the body?
It's the Self.

So you don't need a spaceship.
(Nods)

Do we decide to evolve?
It's human nature. It's also the nature of the universe. Evolution is called Pravritti; *energy flows down and out, expanding and multiplying. The reverse condition, involution, is called* Nivritti; *all energy is withdrawn from the world of objects and is pulled back to its source.*

There is a theory that we are an experiment begun long ago by beings from another planet.
You can also make a theory.

Is Pravritti the downstroke on the cosmic clock — the stage where we experience pleasure and pain?
That is Pravritti, now wind it up. Act just as circus people who first spread their world (Pravritti), and then gather it up (Nivritti). It takes time but it is still Nivritti.

Is there ever a positive time for going with Pravritti?
There are two triangles that symbolize the two states: one pointing down expresses the outward flow of energy, and one pointing upward, expresses the redirection of energy. This is illustrated by a symbol, the six-pointed star, which is made by overlapping the two triangles.

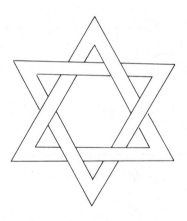

This star is the Yantra (instrument) of Anahata Chakra *(heart center. The process in either direction is the same, but we understand it differently. For example, you marry, build a house, have children, and then gradually reduce your attachments.*

How does one know when his Pravritti is done?
The mind gets a sense, if one has the right samskaras. If not,
Pravritti is limitless.

In the fifth skanda (book) of the Bhagavata Purana there is a
description of the creation of the universe. It shakes me. Is
there any way to understand it besides literally?
Read it in a yogic way: what is Sumeru? *It is the "tenth*
door" or Mula Prakriti. Suppose you are a planet. You have
seven chakras, which are lokas, or universes; seven oceans
around each loka; seven patalas, nether regions. Around each
energy center in your body there are blood vessels; this liquid
equals the oceans. When you understand it is yourself, then
you can apply it to creation outside.

People say the earth plane is all maya. Is there reality here?
Maya is real like a dream is real. When you awake, the dream
is gone.

What remains then?
Truth. The veil over truth is maya.

Is man affected by the planets? If so, how?
Sun, moon, earth, and other planets are all inside of you.
There is no outside except as a projection of inside.

I don't understand how the universe can all fit inside of a
person.
A magnifying glass is so little, but it can make things so big.

Are the chakras like solar systems?
The chakras are called lokas (universes).

Is the universe itself a being?
Inside you there are so many lives, yet you are a being.

71

What chakra are people mostly in?
*All chakras — no one can stay in one state of consciousness.
One who can control the Elements can, but this is in the
immortal stage.*

How about Bhu Loka (Muladhara Chakra, base of the spine)?
*There are four kinds of bliss in the first chakra. We need all
four: spiritual bliss, material bliss, sensual bliss, and the bliss
of wisdom. The first chakra is a reflection of the top
chakra.*

**The universe can play any game with you — everyone has
their own model to play in the universe?**
*Your desire is your world. Every person's world is different.
Each person plays his own game with his desire, or the world.*

I experience out of the body experiences which are new to me.
*They are new because you don't know your past lives. When
we are completely ignorant of our past lives every second is new.*

Does it mean anything to be ignorant of past lives?
It is nature's law.

Is it too "mind blowing" to be aware of all lives?
*Memory is blocked for the purposes of Pravritti, otherwise
creation would stop. The universe is created, and there is a
natural balance to keep it going on. How it keeps in balance
is beyond our mind. If we take a long view we can see the
balance, but at times it seems that bad overpowers good, that
there is more pain than pleasure, and so forth. But no one
can stay the same due to the cycles of the Elements and the
Gunas. A man is a miniature form of the universe, and the
same changes repeat in the universe, but in a larger
framework of time. Although we feel ourselves swinging from
depression to happiness, still the balance remains the same. In
this same way the universe has been going on for an
indefinite period of time.*

People say a pyramid works; some tests show it's not so.
If it is correctly made, it can work.

What is it that works?
It reverses the triangle of Pravritti, which means the loss of energy is stopped.

Are there times when the pyramid manifests more energy than other times?
The full moon, new moons, changes of planets affect it just as they affect mandalas.

Mandalas?
Mandalas are energy instruments and the movement of planets works on mandalas.

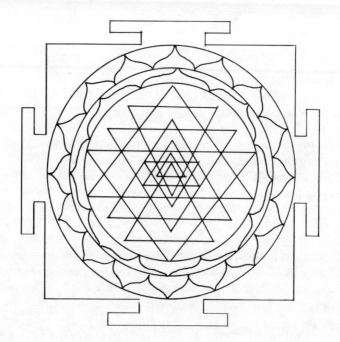

Would you elaborate?

What are mandalas? There is the dot, which is the bindu, *or energy center; the triangle, which represents the three energies, or Gunas; the square which represents the four minds, and the circle, which represents infinity. These things are put in such a way that they can be read.*

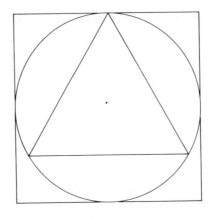

How does the moon affect one?

The moon affects according to its phase, because of its pull on the Water Element.

I find myself in a cycle of being in the here and now, and then another cycle comes when I'm never here now.

This is caused by the change of Elements. The moon affects this change and causes a person to be off balance for several days. There is a method to cure it: plug the right nostril with cotton at sunrise and keep it closed until sunset on those days.

I feel this is a physical answer to a metaphysical question.

The breath is not just physical; it works on the Subtle Body. Changing the breath will change the whole cycle of Elements in the body. The Elements control all thoughts, emotions, actions.

Should one always close the right nostril?
It is normal to have the left nostril open at sunrise, but it gets unbalanced.

During the full moon pressure builds up in my head. What can I do about it?
Fast, by taking one meal a day for four days of Earth predominant foods. Best are those that grow under the ground. Also, take less water.

What happens in crying?
Crying purifies the nerve channels. It takes out excess bile and mucous and strengthens the lungs, but only when a person cries out of positive emotions, not out of anger. There is a Pranayama that does the same purification for those who can't cry. It is called Ujjayi. *All eight sattvic emotions (Ashta Sattvika Vikara) are a natural process for purifying the body. They appear according to the body Humor (Air, Bile, or Mucous) predominant in the person. They are as follows:*

1. Stambha — *stiffness, paralysis*
2. Ashru — *tears*
3. Sveda — *sweat*
4. Kampa — *trembling*
5. Baivarna — *change of color*
6. Svara Bhanga — *cracking of voice*
7. Pulaka — *horripilation, gooseflesh, hair standing on end*
8. Pralaya — *fainting*

What is aura?

Vyana Prana *(one of the five primary subtle energies) spreads through the body and is reflected for four fingers' width around the body. We can all see it and feel it if we try. In meditation this aura can fill the room. Some yogis in jungles appear like balls of light at night.*

Is there a maximum limit to which the human aura can extend?

If a person has a strong will, the aura can extend as far as he can be seen.

With an enlightened being, could it go for miles?

It can. When Hariakhan Baba first appeared in the Hariakhan jungle, he was seen like a star from twelve miles away.

Are there teachers on subtle planes helping us?

The world is a teacher. In the same way all other planes are teachers. To attain a subtle thing we need high consciousness which can be attained by our sadhana, done with faith and devotion.

Do higher minds guide us like intermediaries between ordinary mind and the super-mind (God)?

Higher mind is consciousness. It has several stages. It guides us all the way up to God.

There are seven stages in Yoga sadhana:
1. Desire for enlightenment
2. Attempts to get enlightenment
3. Acquiring one-pointedness   *JIVA STAGE*

4. Self-realization
5. Total non-attachment
6. Absolute non-perception of objects   *DEVA STAGE*

7. Complete isolation   *GOD*

*As long as a person is in the Jiva stage he can't be
non-attached. As soon as he attains the* Deva *(demi-God)
stage he doesn't care about his Gross Body. Then the body
functions by its samskaras and by reflex action. At that stage
one will not remain the doer; so there will be no errors, or
duties, or responsibilities. By the grace of God one can jump
from the third to the fourth stage after several years of
practice. This fourth stage gives him complete knowledge of
the world. Reaching this stage, the Gross Body completes its
life term. One then takes rebirth and starts from the fourth
stage.*

Is there a specific number of souls in the universe?
*If you put one hundred cups of water in the sun, you will see
one hundred suns. The cups can be reduced or increased, but
one sun always exists.*

Mula/Sahasrara

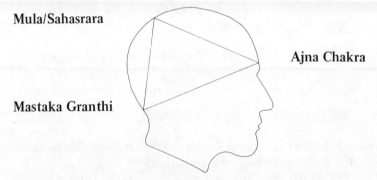

Ajna Chakra

Mastaka Granthi

What is the significance of the number 108?
*There is a triangle made by three points in the head. The path
of Sushumna goes from Mula in Sahasrara, to Ajna Chakra
in the forehead, to* Mastaka Granthi *(head knot) at the base
of the skull.*
*We generally inhale 21,600 times daily. If, by Yoga methods,
we can reduce that number to 108 breaths, the prana stays
within that triangle. At this stage, one is completely
enlightened.*

What is time?
Time is a measurement of distance. Time is made by us. We can change it only as our level of consciousness allows.

Like in dream time?
In a dream one year can be five minutes.

I once dreamt about some events that later came true. How could I have knowledge of the future?
In the superconscious state there is no past, present, or future. What you realized is that everything is inside. This is the realization that comes with Samadhi. In pure dreams it can also be realized. Your dream was due to pure samskaras.

Do you sometimes see the future before you get to it?
Sometimes people get flashes of the future, but when the mind is purified one can see more.

Sometimes I see people and feel like I recognize them, why?
There is no present, only the past is repeating. Don't tell this to people, they will say you're crazy. But try to understand it.

I've read that we're now in Kali Yuga. **What does that mean, and what is the next stage we will go into?**
After Kali Yuga, there is complete destruction. There are four yugas, and each yuga is divided into four parts.

Is Kali Yuga the beginning or the end?
In a circle you can't say what's beginning and what's end.

Can you tell us some of the characteristics of Kali Yuga?
Sat Yuga *is a period of truth;* Treta Yuga *consists of 3/4 truth;* Dvapar Yuga *has 1/2 truth; and* Kali Yuga *has 1/4 truth.*

What's the other 3/4?
Ignorance.

How long do the yugas last?
Enormous periods of time in one sense; in another sense they can be finished by your own efforts. In twenty-four hours, we inhale 21,600 times, and we also exhale the same 21,600 times which equals a total of 43,200 breaths. There are four yugas (ages of man) with a duration ratio of 4:3:2:1. The first, Sat Yuga, lasts four times as long as the last, Kali Yuga. When these numbers (4,3,2,1) are added together they equal ten. If we multiply the 43,200 breaths by ten we get 432,000; this is the length of time in years of the Kali Yuga, which is going on at present. 432,000 times two equals 864,000 years, the age of Dvapar Yuga. 432,000 times three equals 1,296,000 years, the age of Treta Yuga; and 432,000 times four equals 1,728,000 years, the age of Sat Yuga.

In Satya Yuga
Dharma *(the law of truth) remains perfect.*
In Treta Yuga
Dharma is 3/4 predominant and Adharma *(ignorance) is 1/4.*
In Dvapar Yuga
Dharma is 1/2 predominant and Adharma is 1/2.
In Kali Yuga
Dharma is 1/4 and Adharma is 3/4 predominant. (Kalah *means quarrel or tamasic vrittis)*

The total of four yugas, 4,320,000 years, makes one cycle which is called Maha Yuga. *After completion of one cycle, creation disappears and stays in seed form inside Brahma. This rest between cycles is called* Maha Pralaya. *Sometimes* Khanda Pralaya *(partial suspense) prevails and part of the universe disappears, as in the drowning of a continent, or accident, disease, and death in man. All of these yugas are repeated in the individual body and also in the collective body of man. The four stages, Dharma to Adharma, as represented by the yugas, are also present in the same ratio within each yuga. At the present time we are living in the second stage (more or less) of Kali Yuga, which is Tamas Guna predominant, causing quarrels, depression, ego, and so on. But an individual person can get out of this cycle by his own sadhana.*

What can we do to save the planet?
Sit and sing — surrender to God.

RELATIONSHIPS

Regarding relationships, I don't think that anyone can carry one on without taking responsibility for each other for the whole lifetime.

How does one find a soul mate?
The soul never mates, only the samskaras mate. You can say, "samskara mate."

You know what I mean though.
You don't have to look for it. If you were related in previous lives, you will automatically come together. Samskaras get together like grains of sand falling through a sieve. There is no question of choosing.

Can you achieve realization within a marriage relationship?
*Several have attained. Lahiri Mahashaya — Yogananda's
guru's guru — is a perfect example for it. He had several
children, worked in a government job, and still he achieved a
very high state.*

Is solitude preferable to being a householder?
*No, but a householder sometimes needs solitude to see him
or herself from a different angle.*

Is a householder's progress slower?
*Progress depends upon your honesty. A sadhu can be much
slower in sadhana than a householder if he is not honest in
his sadhana.*

**Is any occupation more conducive to sadhana than another,
such as a farmer as opposed to a city dweller, etc.?**
*If a person has work in which he is not dependent on others,
it is better for sadhana.*

**Is there a point in solitude where one can crystalize, where a
person can transcend personal interaction so that one doesn't
need it at all?**
Individually one can. All sadhus are supposed to do that.

You mean there is another world that exists?
It exists inside you.

Should one limit one's friends and relationships?
Socially you should expand.

Is that important?
*Don't consider yourselves sadhus. This creates confusion. We
will talk on a householder level first. After we have talked
about householder life, then those who are exceptions can
ask about sadhu life.*

From letters . . .

Marriage is very important. Although you live together and you have made a child, still there is a thought in the minds of both of you that you are not married. You can't have the real feeling of oneness until you are married.

Surrender of ego to each other is most important. If both wheels of the chariot are not equal then it will not go forward but will go in a circle.

If two wheels of a chariot are not attached to each other then it can't run. Wife and husband need mutual attachment, which is the axle that joins the two wheels. The stronger the attachment, the more the wheels will be together and the smoother they will run. Once you have accepted a mate then always be with him. When water is poured into water both waters become one and can't be separated. Wife and husband are two equal parts of a soybean. One half part of a soybean will not grow. If the two parts are separated and put under the earth, still they will not grow. The bean will grow only when both parts are covered by one skin, which makes two parts as one.

*No one can have everything. We gain something and lose
something. In this way life goes on. Tolerance, compassion,
and contentment — without developing these three qualities
we can't live together and can't love each other. A married
couple should sacrifice their personal desires and row their
boat together. Negativity is not unusual, it exists in everyone.
But we have to overpower these negative things by watching
ourselves. You have made a family. In a family you are free
to do a few things collectively. There is no peace if there is
no limitation of desire.*

*You have known your husband for a long time. If you really
love him, then you have to tolerate a few of his weaknesses
and he has to accept yours. It's a very hard austerity to live
with a person. It needs much sacrifice. If you think you will
get a better person . . . then there is no limit of "better."
You will go on searching and you will not find any 100%
perfect man. So the whole of life will pass away in pain, and
when old age comes you will feel very lonely. In a few cases
it becomes impossible to live together. For example, a
person goes crazy or develops bad habits like drug addiction
or gambling; but if people marry out of real love, they can
adjust and live in harmony for the rest of their lives. When
old age comes they are a support for each other. This is
important because in Western culture young society rejects
old people. Realization of God depends on devotion and faith
toward God. If marriage increases these qualities it can help
toward realization, but if marriage increases worldly desires
it will be a hindrance. We create problems more by our own
dissatisfactions. No one can be happy all the time. Sometimes
a person gets sad and depressed, and at that time his sadness
projects onto the people around him, which creates problems
or dissatisfaction. I have not seen a single householder who
can say that he has no problems. I can't say that
householders can eliminate all problems, but they can reduce
the emotional strain by understanding the real situation.*

When a problem arises it becomes complicated by emotions.
If we think on it peacefully, it can be resolved in some way.

Love and hate are two tendencies of the mind. Because you
say in your mind, "I don't love so and so," you feel hate for
him. If your mind accepts love for him there will be no
problem. It is like self-brainwashing. Your mind is seeking
some more exciting man. This excitement remains for only a
few days, and then the man becomes just like your husband.
Most of the couples in America are facing the same problem.
The result is: marriage, separation, remarriage, reseparation.
The wheel of life is turning in pleasure and pain, and no
peace is ever attained.
Two people can't live together without sacrificing their
personal desires. They are free together, but they are not free
individually. If you look into your past relationships, you
will find that the separation started when one of you started
to be free to satisfy personal desires.

Does separation impede one's inner development?
It depends upon why you marry a person. Is it out of love or simply out of emotion? When romance is finished, everything looks ugly. Marriage and romance are two different things. Separation can, in certain situations, be a tool for growth.

What about duty, the various things we are told. Should one desire pleasure and joy, or forget it and just do our duty?
Bearing the burden of life together peacefully is marriage.

The social duties of a householder are like a weight on my shoulders.
This is your duty and you have to do it happily. You are free to take another path, a hermit's life for example. You are married through your own desires, so you should do your duties happily. No one forced you to get married. You did it through your own desire.

Is it a serious problem for couples to separate?
Separation means running away from the problem.

From letters . . .

*Two different sadhanas are not the real reason for the
problem between you. The reason could be your ego of being
initiated into Tibetan Buddhism and your support of those
ideas in order to pull your wife into it.*

*Spiritual practice is a personal thing. If you both accept one
kind of practice it's OK, and if you don't, still you can
practice in your own ways and live together peacefully. There
is no reason why a wife who is a doctor can't live with her
husband who is a lawyer. They have different trades but it
has no connection with their married life. They can do their
own things separately and live together happily. God is
beyond any name and form and yet has all names and all
forms. You can worship Him in any way. You are initiated
into Tibetan Buddhism, yet you are worshipping the same
God that your wife is worshipping. God is separated in your
minds by your egos. If God is separated, it is an ignorance.
God is in your wife. God is in you. God is in your friends.
God is everywhere. By developing tolerance, compassion, and
contentment, one can worship God truthfully. If these
qualities are not developed, then performing rites and rituals,
Pranayamas, Asanas, meditation, and so forth, will not bring
any result. When a relationship is based on attachment and
competition you can't live together, nor can you leave each
other. One person can't be blamed, because you both are
keeping your male and female egos separate. They are not
dissolving into each other, which makes competition.*

*Yes, there is one sadhana for you both, but it is very difficult.
It needs twenty-four hour awareness. The method is to
develop tolerance, contentment, and compassion. This is the
only way to attain peace and happiness in a relationship.*

*One can be open, loving, and sharing with all and still
maintain the worldly relationships, i.e. brother, sister,
mother, father, husband, friend. To be one with everybody
doesn't mean that you should treat your mother and wife the
same and have sex with both. They are the same in their own
nature but they differ in their relationship to you. When we
say "same," we mean one should not hate one person and
love another person. "Same" doesn't mean that you have to
see their forms the same, their relationship the same. For
example, take a man and a woman. Both are the same in
essence but their functions are different. You can't expect a
man to conceive and give birth to a child, because it is not his
function. You love your husband and you have a particular
bond with him. You love your brother and you have a
different kind of bond with him. In this way all are related in
different ways, but there is one sameness and that is that you
don't hate anyone. Every person in the world is different.
You can't share everything with everybody. This is not
possible.*
You are confusing yourself by mixing sex with love. Love is
a feeling untouched by desires. *This love should be the same
for everyone.*

*Love doesn't come from anywhere. It is already in us. When
the mind is purified, then the heart opens up. As long as the
mind is not pure then real love can't manifest. But if a person
is in the process of purifying the mind, which means
reduction of hate, then love will start growing. Reduction of
negative qualities or developing positive qualities are not two
different things. The monks in solitude try to control their
negative qualities, and when they overpower their negative
qualities they come out of solitude. They don't have to go
to the public to show love or compassion, but love shines by
itself.*

What is the difference between divine and personal love?
Divine love is not polluted by desires. Personal love is mixed with attachment.

Can't personal love be divine too?
Personal love minus attachment equals divine love.

How can we deal with the pain of loving someone who can't accept our love?
If a candle is lit it spreads its light. If love is inside it will spread by itself. There is no question of acceptance or rejection. If love is mixed with some kind of attachment, it is a different kind of love — it is controlled by selfishness, possessiveness, and other desires. In such cases you can't force love on someone. It is not natural love.

From letters . . .

You cannot compare your having two men with a mother who has two babies, because it is a different kind of relationship. It's the same kind of argument as, "A man's wife is a woman, and his mother is also a woman, so what's the harm of his having sex with his mother?" I can't agree with such arguments.
The wife and husband relationship is not only physical. It is a relationship with pure love. They sacrifice their personal desires to maintain their love and their relationship. Marital sex is not a physical thing. It is a very important part of love. It should be considered as sacred as love for God. *If a person wishes only to fulfill the sensual desires with another person, then it doesn't matter with whom he or she lives. It's not love. You can say one man with two wives is equally as bad as one woman with two husbands. I accept it; it's a correct argument. I am not telling you to change your desires. But I'll say that there is no end to desire. A person who is in the habit of eating varieties of food always remains hungry. There is no contentment even though the person eats food and enjoys it. He still craves some new thing. There is no limit, and if the desires are not limited there will be no peace. If parents are not in peace the children will get their samskaras, and then their lives will become painful when they begin to understand the world.*

In marriage it is difficult if one partner wishes to be celibate and the other does not. You both have to decide about it. I believe sex is a sacred part of love and can't be shared with everybody. The wife/husband relationship is right for sharing sex because they took a vow to be one.

91

It is always upsetting for a woman to see her husband with other women. Also, if a man is honest, it is upsetting for him if his wife goes to other men. If wife and husband agree to be free to have sex with others, they don't get upset, but they don't love each other. They simply live together like two unknown people. They don't relate to each other spiritually and emotionally. It is the reason that ages ago wise people made a rule of a one-to-one relationship.

A woman who loves her husband can't and shouldn't tolerate possession of her husband by any other woman. A saint once sang a song which means, "The lane of love is so narrow that only two can walk at a time."

No one can have peace if sensual desires are not put under a limit. The family system is for limiting sensual desires. One husband, one wife, and their children make a family. If this one-to-one relationship is rejected, then the mind will always search for new relationships, and this desire will never end. Some day the old body will be thrown into an old people's home, incapable of fulfilling sensual desires, but with the mind full of desires. This is the greatest pain in life. A mind full of sensual desires doesn't accept aging. This non-acceptance creates much pain in old people. They die in pain and develop samskaras of pain due to not being capable of fulfilling desires.

The best thing for attaining peace is to keep the desires within a limit and accept yourself. Accept the wife and husband relationship. Accept old age, and accept death. This acceptance will stop making new samskaras. There will be contentment in life, and contentment is peace, love, God.

I always have a vague anxiety — maybe I'm fearful that my relationship won't last.
When there are several expectations and we don't get those expectations fulfilled we create a feeling of unhappiness. If there is love, and expectations can be kept within a limit, you will see there is no pain or feeling of abandonment.

Many of us seem to be searching for a way to fill emptiness through pleasure.
What is emptiness? You have lost the quality of love so you try to fill the gap. There must be mutual love and a sense of surrender to each other in marriage. Otherwise it will be very painful for both.

Female and male are two energies that need the support of each other. These two energies reinforce each other and grow together. This is the process of Nature. But human consciousness is much higher than that of other natural beings. Human beings seek a particular type of love in each other, and when they find that love they become one, inseparable. Even the separation of bodies by death can't separate that love. Yoga means union of God with Jiva, which can also be called male and female energies. So by true love one can also unite with God. God is everywhere and in everything. If we truly reach out for God in one thing — in love, in art, in devotion, in Yoga — then we can reach the real truth.

PREGNANCY

The desire for reproduction is mainly in the female, which is natural. Your desire to have a baby is a reality. Your body is made for that. The sexual union of male and female is for reproduction. If you are attached to each other, what difference will it make if you are attached to your own seed also?

The world is overpopulated, it's true, but a couple can replace themselves by making two children. In this way the population will always remain the same. If a person is afraid of taking responsibility for children, then he is not doing his duty for the world. If both male and female agree not to have babies and live like hermits, that's another thing. But from a biological point of view your desire to have a baby is natural, and your husband should respect your desire.

Does a couple's consciousness at the time of conception determine the consciousness of the child?
The child gets some of the samskaras of the parents.

How does that affect the child?
If the parents have anger or hate at the time, the child will get those samskaras. If they are in a higher, loving space the child will have a more loving nature.

Is it OK for a woman to get pregnant if she knows she won't be living with the father?
What do you think?

I don't know. I am confused about it.
A baby without a father is not accepted by this society. Animal behavior cannot be copied in human society. You have made a family system, and for a family, male energy is very important.

I don't know how to undo the harm of negative emotions that I put on my unborn child.
First, don't worry yourself by thinking of the negative things you have done. Do positive things now.

How do negative emotions affect the unborn child?
After three to four months, the fetus develops emotions and can feel the negative or positive emotions of the mother.

Does the parent's negativity have permanent effects on the child?
It makes a print on the mind of the unborn child — makes a tendency in the child to behave in a certain way, which can be permanent.

How will a child, or anyone, overcome them?
By giving the child love. You have to understand the cause, and then put positive things into the mind.

What about abortion?
It is killing. But when you control the death rate, then you have to control the birth rate.

Is birth control bad?
Self control is better than birth control.

It's harder!
Nothing is easy.

Chinese say the soul enters the child two hours after birth. What do they say in India?
Twenty-two days after conception. Life is already there but the soul enters in twenty-two days. The emotions and the mind develop after four months.

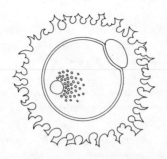

Your depression, sadness, pain are part of your pregnancy.
Even though you had an abortion, still the full effect of the
pregnancy is not gone. Pregnancy is not only physical, it is
emotionally connected with the Subtle Body. That is why
the mother develops love for the baby, even if it is not born.

During pregnancy a woman should avoid hard physical labor,
physical discomfort, indulgence in grief, fright, and so forth.
As soon as a woman conceives, her attachment also
conceives. This attachment creates a feeling of protection for
the fetus she is carrying.
In the first month of pregnancy all the five Elements (Earth,
Water, Fire, Air and Ether) make a gelatinous substance and
become condensed by the action of the three Humors —
Mucous, Bile, and Air.
From the second to third month five lumps appear at the
places of the five extremities — head, arms, and legs.
In the fourth month, the limbs become more developed;
and the emotional heart, the seat of consciousness, appears
(this is not the physical heart which develops in the first
weeks). So from the fourth month a baby develops desires of
taste, smell, touch, which appear through the longings of its
mother. At that time if the desires of a mother are not
gratified it can affect the growth of a child.

In the fifth month a fetus develops Manas (Mind) and wakes up from the sleep of its subconscious existence. In the sixth month Buddhi (Intellect) comes in. The fetus develops its proper shape. In the womb the child feels pain and discomfort, but it's all like a dream as when something is felt in a semi-conscious state.

It's useless to worry about whether a child feels pain or pleasure inside the womb, because it's the law of nature that everyone must pass through those stages. God has made a system of nature in which everything is controlled. If suffering comes, then a strength to tolerate it also comes. If a child in the womb suffers certain kinds of pain, there definitely develops some kind of pranic energy which gives him strength of tolerance.

Read scriptures and stories about saints. This is also a sadhana. It makes good samskaras in the mind of a baby. After the fourth month a pregnant woman is conscious of two hearts — her own heart and the baby's heart. Her awareness is directly connected with the baby inside her womb, through the umbilical cord. This relationship of mother and child is the highest of all physical relationships. God's creation is also God. So everything is God. Worship His creation, admire the beauty of it, and be happy.

According to the law of nature there is no choice of having or not having children. When we adopt an unnatural life, then we say, "I'll have children," or "I don't want to have children."

The baby takes birth in the world by his own samskaras; and then the parents pass on their samskaras; and then those of friends, relatives, society — all kinds of samskaras — fill the baby. It's like filling an empty bag with all kinds of garbage. But the baby is capable of emptying the bag at any age in his life. Although it is also by his own samskaras that

*he may want to get rid of that "garbage." No one can remain
a new born baby. Even the high reincarnated saints get
samskaras and act according to them: just as Rama was sent
to the jungle and separated from his wife; Krishna was
separated from his gopis and fought battles; Buddha left his
palace and faced so much pain and troubles; Jesus was
crucified. Nature is a huge machine. It is so perfect that it
keeps the balance of births and deaths. Earthquakes, floods,
famines, diseases, wars are the natural means of controlling
the population. If the earth is overfilled with living beings,
then something will happen and the population will reduce.
It doesn't make any difference if a part of the earth drowns
in the ocean; somewhere a new earth will come up when it is
needed. In the same way, if a person doesn't want to have
children, then someone else will give birth in twos, threes, or
fours.
A newborn baby is the purest form of a human being. This
purity remains until the baby understands my/mine,
you/yours.*

*Yes, men relate to women with sex desire. Also women relate
to men with the same thought. There is no end to it. The
more a person gives freedom to sex desire, the more it comes.
And then what happens? Like a deer running after a mirage,
the result is to die of thirst. Those men, who relate to you
with sex desire, relate to other women in the same way. So
their desire jumps from one woman, to another woman, and
another woman; and when they get old the senses become
incapable of enjoying sex, but the desire still jumps and it is
the worst pain in life.
I have seen people who tried free sex and they are not happy.
I have seen people who are celibate, they are not happy
either. I have seen householders living in a one-to-one basis,
they are unhappy too. So what is the answer to attain*

happiness? The answer is to live by keeping limits on desires. It is hard tapas. One has to observe strict discipline made by himself. One who can do that can lead a happy life.

Wife and husband relationship includes all relationships — master/servant, parent/child, teacher/student, friends, and sexual partner. If one is in pain the other at once helps by taking the position of teacher, master, parent — whatever is needed. This is the beauty of the wife and husband relationship. If these supports are lacking, it is not a real marriage.

The two of you are living together. Whenever one gets pain and depression the other should help. It's like two people rowing the same boat. If one gets tired the other helps, and sometimes both row together to reach the goal faster. There is a mutual understanding that they both depend on each other's energy, cooperation, and love.

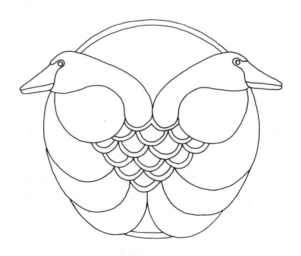

There is a story of a swan who had two heads. The swan could eat food much faster than other one-headed swans. One day the two heads began to argue about which one ate faster and which one was slower. After a heated argument they began to hate each other. One head found a poison berry and said to the other head, "I can't live with you any longer," and picked up the poison. The other head said, "Wait, don't eat it! If you eat I'll also die." But the other head was so angry that he swallowed the poison anyway, and thus died the two-headed swan.

Among 90% of householders this kind of argument is going on, and instead of compromising they separate.

Children copy their parents, friends, and teachers. They will develop the habits of their parents and friends. So if you want your child to be honest, peaceful, and happy you should be that way first. Spanking a child can train him — like an animal in the circus he will do as you say without understanding why. The best thing is to make children understand what is right and what is wrong. But when you, yourself, act with different kinds of emotions and project your anger onto your child, how can you tell him what is wrong? Again, you have to understand your emotions first.

There is a difference of age and energy between a child and his parents. Parents should always keep this difference in mind. Because they can't scream, run, and jump like a child, they can't tolerate a child running and jumping, and they use anger to try to stop him. When a child's energy is stopped by force he develops frustration and he revolts against his parents. Children should play together, and if your child learns some bad things, then tell him it is not good. He will obey you, if you are honest with him.

What do you think of the commandment to honor thy father and mother?
They are the first gurus.

Doesn't parenthood create attachment? Is that good?
Attachment is necessary for the needs of nature, survival of the species. But dispassion can also arise from the relationship. For example, when a son abuses his father, the father at once gets dispassion. Father is attached to the son and when the child abuses him he sees that his son can't bring him peace, and he gets dispassion. Or selfless service to children can cultivate the qualities of tolerance, compassion, and contentment which can bring dispassion.

Did you say householders must have attachments?
With understanding. I am attached to this chalkboard. I'll not cry if it breaks, but I'll keep it safe. Householders can't say, "I'm unattached," and let children play in the street and get killed by a car.

Can parents be less attached when children are older?
Your duty changes; it changes the nature of attachment.

Can you say something about right attitude with children?
Become a child. A teacher when teaching a child to add, counts on his fingers as the child does.

How to become a child?
If you love them it's easy. You were and are a child. A tree grows from a seed and the tree never separates from the seed. We don't have to pretend to be a child; that nature is always in us.

How do you know what is your duty when disciplining a child? When do you spank him, and so on?
Discipline yourself first and he will come around. He's your mirror.

In handling my child, I don't know when to give in and when to discipline.
A mother knows instinctively.

But I'm not in touch with my instincts.
Don't depend on others and books, then you will know. How do tribal mothers know?

Can you be more explicit about how duty changes?
You don't treat your sixteen year old daughter as a child.

It is hard to know when I am doing my duty and when I am treating her as a child.
That is attachment without understanding.

Can you speak about duty of children to parents?
Children's duty is to copy the parents.

What is parent's duty to children?
To take care of them. If you take good care, they will copy you.

Is it ever the duty of children to care for the parents?
It's their duty if they learned it from their parents. If you take care of your mother, your daughter will take care of you.

I teach small children in school, and I worry about competition. It seems bad for them.
Competition is bad only if it stops the growth of the losers and they develop a fear to stand by themselves. On the other hand competition encourages children to develop their physical and mental strength. If there is no competition there is no fun for children. You should not worry about competition, but you should encourage the losers separately. Competition to hurt others by thought, act, or words is bad and should not be encouraged. If there is a competition between two groups then one child will not have to take the responsibility for losing and will not develop fear. One-to-one

*competition can harm the loser very much. The group should
be changed all the time so that they will not develop a
feeling of group separatism. We learn by using our senses
properly. The most important thing to teach children is to
use their senses properly. Really hearing, looking, touching,
smelling, tasting is a real knowledge. One who has learned
this can attain any worldly knowledge easily.*

How do you teach children to meditate?
Meditate yourself and they will copy you.

Children are pure, can we keep them that way?
No, the world pollutes.

Are children established in witness-consciousness?
As long as they don't recognize the world.

How young can a child be to read scriptures with understanding?
*It depends on the child's samskaras. Some can understand
from an early age, some can't. They can read through the
actions of the parents. Reading a book is not important. You
can explain things in your own language, you don't need to
quote scriptures.*

Why do parents disapprove of a spiritual leader? Why do they want their child to come to them instead of to a leader?
*It's a fear of losing possession of a child. Also there is an age
difference in parents and children, so a child can't relate to
them openly. They can relate to others because there they
don't consider the difference of age. All parents want their
children to become like Jesus, Buddha or other famous
saints, but they don't want them to face the hardships Jesus
and Buddha faced.*

BRAHMACHARYA

Is sexual continence necessary for sadhana? Is the purpose of it to preserve one's semen?
Bindu (semen) is vital energy. In its purest form it is called
Ojas. *This Ojas has tremendous power and can go straight up to the top of Sahasrara. But a person who is moderate in his sexual behavior is also classified as a* Brahmachari.

What is moderate behavior?
The male and female sexual act is natural once a month. If this is reduced even more it is better for sadhana. People here think much on sex, that's why they are more trapped. Even sex can be used as a method of Yoga, if it is not on the physical level.

It's difficult to attain sexual dispassion. To center on a higher level while engaging in sex seems contradictory.
It's very difficult. Sex is one of the natural tendencies. It can be transcended or eliminated very slowly. Practice very slowly. Otherwise the mind will revolt.

What if the mind is in the habit of revolting?
Imprison it!

What is the role of sex in spiritual life?
Kundalini is sex energy. When its flow is channeled upward, it opens all energy centers and eventually brings enlightenment. In Tantric Yoga, the method is to use sex as a means of controlling the flow of the energy. But in certain Tantric practices loss of semen is dangerous. Normally a person should keep to a middle path, which can also open up the energy centers.

What is the middle path just mentioned?

Moderate sex. Once a month is yogic moderation for married people. Kundalini is female. When its flow is toward the world (pravritti-evolution) it is called sex desire, and when its flow is upward (nivritti-involution) it is called awakening of Kundalini. The physical sensations as it flows in either direction are the same. So when Kundalini is vibrated, any of many emotions, including sex desire, may arise. At this point a person should not be afraid of sexual desire, but should watch this change. A man has the ego of masculinity so he feels the femininity of Kundalini. If he can imagine that God is masculine, and that all of us — men and women — are feminine lovers of God, then his ego of masculinity will disappear and he won't be lost in sex desire. This was the attitude of Ramakrishna Paramahansa.

Brahmacharya is the same for men and women? What about loss of fluid?

Semen is energy in both sexes; fluid is its gross form. The rules are the same for men and women. Women also have semen which is called Raja.

Is it possible to control sexual sensation through Mantra?

Not Mantra, but mind.

But doesn't sex also generate energy?

Yes, it generates and makes a child.

What is the difference between abstinence and Brahmacharya? What does Yoga do to change that energy? What practices transmute sexual energy?

What is important is preserving semen as a vital fluid. Abstaining from sex doesn't mean celibacy; the desire for sex must be transcended. If one is trying to stop and still gets thoughts of sex, that is OK; it is only natural. There are specific practices to preserve semen. Pranayama is the best

method. A few Asanas are also for that. For Westerners
Brahmacharya is almost impossible because association
between sexes is so free. But a person can be enlightened
without Brahmacharya if sex is lived in a natural way. Don't
mix the sadhu trip in this thing, because there are different
rules for sadhus. People read books, then try to follow rules
and go crazy. Those rules are for hermits.

Maybe it depends on how you are happiest?
What is happiness? Follow simple rules and don't go to
extremes.

Psychology talks about sex repression and its bad effects.
What is not sex? Our energies are passing from one person to
another right here. We don't have the same energy, any of us.
But when we are together it passes naturally. According
to Tantra, Brahmacharya is not abandonment of sex but
transcendence of it.

**Is there an evolutionary reason for increased sex in our
culture?**
The more the mind is developed, the more it will search for
sensual pleasures. You have sexual freedom, but people are
still trying to search more pleasure. They are experimenting
with different ways, and still they are discontented. This
discontentment leads to violence and sexual perversion.

Brachmacharya is a very big word. One who is on the path of Brahma (God) is a Brahmachari. Its main purpose is to control desire and retain bindu, which is a very powerful energy. Married people who limit their sexual desires are Brahmacharis.

In ancient times all saints were householders. They would have children, and also they would do Yoga. But in their mind Yoga was real and reproduction was only a play of nature.

From letters . . .

Sex is an addiction. The more you do, the more you want to do. It's like a dog chewing a dry bone. His gums bleed and he feels the taste of blood and thinks the bone is tasty.
It's your own blood that gives you pleasure. If you get pleasure by discharging semen, you can get several times more pleasure by storing semen. It's not easy, but also it's not impossible. The best way is to gradually reduce the loss of semen.

There is no difference if a person falls from the top of a tree or from the top of a rock — he will get hurt either way. Losing semen by homosexuality, heterosexuality, or masturbation are the same, because the loss of semen is the same. Time is going and not coming. Every second of your life is going. Your life will get shorter whether you do good things or bad things. But if you do good things, you will gain good things like happiness, peace, bliss. If you do bad things you will gain bad things, like anger, hate, jealousy, fear. In both cases loss of life is inevitable, but the attainment is different. For example, two travelers go to Mt. Shasta. One goes while singing, playing, and enjoying nature; the other goes quarreling with people, being angry, and afraid. Both reach Mt. Shasta, but one's heart blooms like a lotus and the other's heart pops like a balloon.

Do you know that February and March, September and October, when the sun changes its position, these four months increase the emotions and people develop craziness, anger, and increased sex desire? By doing regular sadhana one can keep the mind in balance.

Sexual perversion develops due to fear. When a person can't relate to another on the sexual level without fear, his mind naturally develops perversion.

Homosexuality is an addiction just like other sexual acts. Society doesn't accept it for various reasons. The union of male and female is natural for reproduction. As it is considered natural, the social structure is based on this union. If the whole country becomes homosexual, then what will be the shape of society? It is not possible, but society has discouraged homosexuality because of the fear that it will destroy the structure.
This discouragement creates a guilt feeling in homosexuals. Even if no one tells them it is wrong, still they feel guilty. If you want to stop it, then don't do it. If you want to do it, then don't feel guilty about it.
Addictions can be switched. It takes time to forget one addiction and get hooked into another addiction. If you really want to change yourself, then be celibate for three months, and after three months have a relationship with a woman who really wants to help you. If you live with a member of the opposite sex a new energy can be created by the union of male and female energies.

The world is an abstract art. We all see in it what we want to see. There is a mixture of good and bad and both are important for making the wheel of nature move. There can't be a day if there is no night. For some, day is good, and for some, night is good. The main thing is to make the present peaceful. Forget the past and don't think on the future; the future is based on the present. If the present is peaceful, then gradually the future will be peaceful.

Life is not a burden. We make it a burden by confusing ourselves, by thinking on the past and making plans for the future, and not thinking of the present.

You are in the mountains where there is fresh air and water, where there are trees and plants and streams. Sit with them and enjoy the creation of God. God and His creation are not separate.

111

Desire makes desire and in this way the whole world is formed. This spider web of desire is inside us and spreads outside. Just like a spider, we weave the web and we can also swallow it.

DESIRES

A saint lived in a jungle. One day another saint came and gave
him a book, the Bhagavad Gita. The saint would read the
book daily. One day he saw the book had been chewed by
rats. He decided to keep a cat to prevent the rats. He kept a
cat, but a cat needs milk to drink. So he kept a cow. Now he
could not look after all these animals by himself so he
engaged a woman to look after the cow. After two years in
that jungle there was a big house, his wife, two babies, cats,
cows and everything. Now the saint became worried. He
thought about how happy he had been when he was alone.
Now instead of thinking about God, he was thinking about
his wife, kids, cow, and cats. He began to ponder on how it all
happened, and he came to the conclusion that one tiny book
had made such a big world.

Where does desire originate?

The desires we get are actually samskaras. They are formed this way:

1. *Having union with an object, possessing it.*
2. *The object is not present, but stays in the mind.*
3. *A craving for the object is created.*
4. *The craving makes a print on the mind which remains after death (samskara).*

Desire is the third stage. We don't feel the first two stages, they are too subtle. Samskaras recreate desires in the next birth automatically. A person can get the desire to steal although brought up in a good family. He himself can't understand why he desires it. These desires develop more when they are fulfilled. Desires can be overcome by controlling them; we have to put a limit on desires.

Do desires eventually stop leaving an imprint on the mind?

Desires will change into desire for attaining God instead of the world.

Aren't we born to experience these desires?

Desire and the world are the same thing. We make this world by our desires and we are capable of finishing it. But it is not easy to do unless we develop extreme dispassion. For developing dispassion, we have to play all those tricks called Yoga.

Must you let go of compassion to have dispassion?

There are three stages: passion — desire for sensual objects; compassion — desire for helping others; dispassion — beyond both. There are three ways of playing life's game: first, with passion, which starts as soon as discrimination develops, very young in life. If this stage doesn't change into compassion we are playing only one game in life; but it changes, more or less, in every person. Next, we develop compassion by using the same discriminating mind. And finally, compassion is the foundation for dispassion.

116

What is the relationship of passion to love?
Passion is completely related to the senses, and love is related to the pureness of heart.

And compassion?
Compassion is the desire to help others. It is still related to the senses. But dispassion is beyond both passion and compassion. When faith, devotion, and right thinking are developed it is called vairag, *a stage of dispassion. A person gets dispassion from the world because his high consciousness makes him understand that the world is an illusion or maya. One who doesn't identify himself with the sensual object is unattached, desireless, and contented. Attachment is a rope which binds the desires and sensual objects (the world) together.*

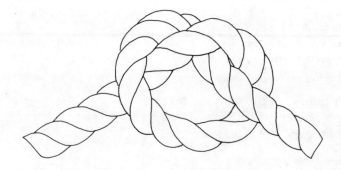

Why should we avoid desires if we don't hurt anyone else or ourselves?
Desire makes desire. It has no limit. When desires are limited it gives peace.

Can we free ourselves from desires through acting them out but watching them happen?
There is desire with attachment and desire without attachment, which is called dispassion. No one can be totally desireless — we are alive because we desire to live. Be in your desire without desire.

How can one know which desires to act on and which just to watch?
Some desires are important to keep the body fit to live, fit for society, such as food. Some desires are not important but they possess our minds very much in order to please the senses. We should watch those desires.

Somehow, living on this planet with this body, I feel these senses should be pleased.
Senses can be pleased by drugs, and drugs can kill the senses. But if we use our senses in the right way we can be happy in the world.

Other things . . . the opposite sex . . .
What is the limit? You have to keep a limit in order to enjoy sex, otherwise it will also kill you.

But if you have a desire for something . . .
Switch the mind or learn by burning the fingers that fire is hot.

How do we get rid of our desires?
Desire is life. If there are no desires at all, then we can't move in the world. Poison in a proper dose cures a disease, but if taken in an overdose it kills. Desire kills when you are trapped in desire. Your few needs are natural and a few desires are not important. You can reduce them naturally.

All great men have had the desire to achieve. Without this desire they would not have done anything. What about this?
That desire was important because first they made an aim and then dissolved themselves to follow that aim. You can't work without desire.

People say one should rid himself of desire. But what if desire is for God?
That is devotion, not desire. Desire to seek truth is a sattvic desire — spiritual desire is part of truth.

Desire makes the object, all of the objects that are in your life. The only escape from the trap is to realize that the objects and conditions of your life come out of you, that they are illusions projected by you. So why identify with them?

How do we get bad habits?

We get good and bad habits in two ways, by samskaras and from our environment. Samskaras are the impressions of the actions of past lives; it is very difficult to have any control over such habits unless we build a very strong will power by doing hard tapas. Our environment includes the time a baby is in the womb and receiving the emotions of the mother; when he takes birth; when he copies his parents, neighbors, friends, society, and so on. The second type of habit which we form is not difficult to break; as soon as we understand that this habit is wrong we can stop it. But a bad habit which is formed by samskaras is very dangerous. For example, a person loves killing. It gives him pleasure. He cannot stop it because he is guided by his samskaras. By his wrong actions he builds more samskaras, and in this way he degenerates to an animal level.

What is good and bad? Aren't they the same?

On one level there is no good and bad, but as long as you have to question, you are on the level of good and bad.

Good and bad samskaras are like seeds of different plants kept in a bottle: some grow in winter, some in the summer, and some in the rainy season. If you throw all the seeds on the earth, the seed which grows in that season will grow and the others will remain dormant. Exactly the same thing happens with samskaras. All kinds of samskaras are there but they grow according to the person, place, or thing with which we associate. If we go with depraved people, the bad samskaras will automatically come up and good samskaras will remain dormant. If we sit with a truthful person, samskaras of truthfulness will automatically come up. A human being is not entirely bound by samskaras, otherwise it would be useless to try to attain enlightenment.

Why are we so attached to the physical plane if it is illusion?
*The attachment is also illusion. Because nature is evolution it
needs attachments.*

Why are we separated from God?
*When a human being takes birth and develops the mind, he
experiences the pleasure of the world, that is sensual
pleasure. In the next birth the sensual desires increase, and in
the next, they increase more. It's like a flow of water which
runs downward. It helps reproduction and the continuation
of the world and at the same time it puts a curtain between
the jiva and God.*

**Is it because the Lord wants it to happen? Is He the guy
making the trouble?**
*He is not making the trouble, we are making the trouble. He
gives us food but we overeat.*

What is pleasure and what is pain?
*A kind of understanding accepted by the mind is called
pleasure, and when that understanding is rejected by the
mind it changes to pain. Pleasure and pain are self-created
illusions. Because the world itself is an illusion, we have to go
through all these pleasures and pains to attain the truth. When
pleasure continues for a time it gives a feeling of happiness.
But there is no real pleasure in this world. Material
possessions can't protect one from pain. Desire, attachment,
and pain keep the machine of the world running. If these
stopped, everything would stop and the world would be dead.*

Why does a person become discontented?
*Discontentment is created by non-fulfillment of desires. It
takes various forms, but the three primary expressions of it
are eating, possessiveness, and attachment. As soon as a being
takes birth he wants to eat, so eating is the first natural
tendency in a being. But when he develops a sense of*

121

discentment he begins to eat without considering his needs and that is called gluttony.

The second natural tendency in a being is to own the object his senses are attracted to. When he develops a sense of discontentment he wants more and more things, which is called possessiveness. It is a feeling of closeness with an object and a sense of ownership. When the senses are attracted to an object the mind develops attachment to it and thus loses its discriminative power, which creates delusion. This delusion wipes out all memory of a higher Self and makes ignorance, which causes lust, covetousness, aggression, anger, envy, jealousy, and hate.

The veil comes like this:

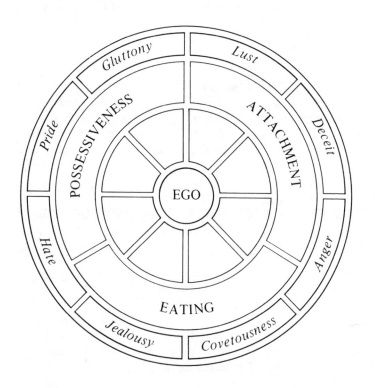

The search for liberation begins by developing contentment which controls these eight demons. When all these demons are controlled, then automatically desires are controlled. When desires are controlled, the ego of existence is eliminated and a being becomes immortal.

Why is there pain in this world?
If you think deeply on this you will come to the conclusion that it exists because we search for pleasure. The mind compares, "This is pleasure, and this is pain." Pleasure and pain are nothing but the acceptance and rejection of the mind.

Anger has three forms: hate, hostility, and fear. The root cause of it is attachment. The world would not exist without attachment, and it is present in everyone to a greater or lesser degree.

Is there a way to express negative qualities through sadhana?
What kind of negative quality?

Anger.
Hold the breath several times, the anger will go away.

What is the difference between controlling anger and supressing it?
When you accept it, you control it; when you don't accept, but don't show it, then it's suppressing.

How can you express anger without hurting? What do you do with angry energy?
You should dissolve it. As long as you don't accept it, then you can't get rid of it.

Is this true with fear?
What is fear? Fear is the brother of anger. When you accept fear, you will understand why you are afraid. Anger is a weapon for self-protection. Sometimes we do it for protection from our own guilt. If you accept anger, why feel guilty afterwards? Jealousy and guilt feelings are still part of anger.

So you are not really accepting anger if you still have feelings of guilt and jealousy?
Anger is not a small thing. It comes out with different faces — resentment, for example. But you think only screaming is anger.

When I get angry I start to express it and I cry.
That is also a face of anger. You can smile too, and still be angry.

So if a saint controls his desires he will also control anger and fear?
As soon as fear is gone, the stage comes called nirdvandva, *fearlessness, the highest stage of a saint.*

How can I learn to forgive someone who has hurt me?
Don't forgive, forget. Forgiving means that you still have anger.

What is the best way to deal with my anger?
By being aware of it: "I am angry." Accept this condition.

What if I am still angry after acceptance?
Then you won't hit anyone. Gradually it will go away.

You think if you are aware, you won't hit anyone?
That's right. When we are not aware of it, then we go mad.

I have the same question about self-pity and grief involved with anger. Is it dishonest to pacify it or suppress it?
Anger and fear are two sides of the same coin. Why does a person become angry? Because he is afraid and wants to protect himself. If you have no fear, you will not be angry. Self-pity and grief are forms of fear.

Is working with fear a long term process? What about the present?
When an aspirant wants to keep himself free from anger, hate, and fear, these devils attach themselves more and sometimes create a kind of madness in the mind. For that, satsanga is very important. Satsanga means association with those who are truth seekers. If you confess your hidden, bad emotions to your associates they will go away. If it comes up again do the same thing. Identify the problem, don't reject it. When you recognize the bush, the bear disappears.

How can I plug into the energy I know is there?
The flow of energy in the body is blocked when the mind indulges in anger, hatred, and selfishness. Keep your mind pure and you will see how easily the energy moves.

Can negative emotions be useful?
Like what?

Negative effects of the moon or other things — negative emotions, or what makes them happen, how do I deal with them?

Negative emotions can come by negative conditions of the body, such as sickness, or by the environment, or by samskaras. The Elements and the environment can be changed easily, but change of samskaras can be very difficult. The moon affects the Water Element primarily; it can be changed. Cut down on water intake, eat more root foods, and don't sleep during the night of the full moon or the next day. If you're in a bad environment, change the place. To wipe out bad samskaras, you have to do sadhana.

Is happiness peace?
No. In happiness the mind is engaged with the object of happiness, while in peace there is no object, no thought, just peace.

Does pain come from trying to hang onto things, accustomed ways of life?
Non-acceptance of life is pain. For instance, when one gets older and does not accept age, there is pain.

Yes. But is there not an easy way to get out of pain?
By acceptance. It's only a matter of switching the mind.

How does one understand on more than an intellectual level?
Intellectual understanding is like seeing New York on a map. You have to be there to feel it. For that one needs sadhana.

When I was twenty-two I lost the sight in my right eye. I wonder if this affects my inner vision, how I see myself?
No. The inner vision is never affected if the outer eye gets some defect.

I listen better with my eyes closed.
Because you have fear, you close your eyes when someone talks to you.

Why do we hang onto fear?
People like the pain of a thorn in the foot. But you haven't disclosed the real problem that is bothering you.

Would expressing it make it go away?
It helps understanding. When you don't express it, it is like putting ash over the fire; the fire goes on burning inside.

I could relate twenty-five or more problems but . . .
Separation from a man is causing your pain and disclosing all of your non-acceptances.

How do I learn to accept myself?
You know you can't have a younger body. You can accept this fact either painfully or cheerfully.

127

Yes. It's as simple as that.

Cheerfulness is a happiness inside the heart related to contentment

I think of myself as a compassionate and tolerant person, but I am not contented.

They are three masks of the one thing. A discontented, compassionate person is an impossibility.

How can I do the work I do without feeling resentment and frustration?

If one thinks the burden of the world is on his shoulders then he begins to feel the burden, and in a few years he becomes hunchbacked. Then one day he realizes that the world is existing by itself. But it's too late, the hunchback can't be straightened. You have your duties and responsibilities for the world, and you can either accept them with a smile or you can reject them with tears. It doesn't make any difference to the world, but it makes a difference in your feelings. 90% of pain is self-created. It can be removed by understanding that there is no real cause of pain.

A person should think all his actions are for God. So your garden is for God, you eat for God, and your life is for God. When this thought becomes deeper you will find that God is everywhere and all your actions are meditation. Gradually the chains of anger, hate, jealousy will loosen, and one day you will be free and fly away.

I do sadhana regularly but still feel depressed, why?
*I don't think it's a new thing in human nature to develop
sadness and depression. According to Yoga, one Element
predominates for an hour in the body. When either Air or
Ether Element predominates it makes sadness and depression,
and when Earth or Water predominates it keeps the mind
calm and happy. But those who have attained higher stages
in Yoga can be helped by Air and Ether Elements. All yogis
pass through this stage of depression, but when their sadhana
goes higher they get control over it. Due to worldly
attachment and hidden desires, this depression increases.
Yoga sadhana can give you the ability to understand what is
causing the unhappiness. Yoga is a very hard path. So when
the worldly desires come, don't be disheartened. Let them
come and then reflect that desire increases by fulfillment,
and dies out of nonfulfillment. A man can't fulfill his desires
forever. Every desire is like a fire, the more fuel you give to it
the more it will increase. Life is full of tides, like an
ocean . . . everyone's boat goes up and down.*

What is guilt?

When a person accepts that his actions were wrong.

What is the medicine for guilt?

There is only one medicine. Do sadhana and look forward. If you climb a pole you have to look to the top. Guilt is nothing. We make it to hide. We say, "I am feeling guilty," but again repeat the same deed that gave us guilt. If we don't repeat, then no guilt.

I understand your inferiority complex. It can be cured if you try to get out of it. But most people like the pain of a thorn in their foot.

Before doing Yoga, you have to make up your mind that you don't want to live in the confusion of your thoughts, which cover your mind like a tangled web of barbed wire. The next thing is to open yourself by playing, singing, dancing. In the beginning people are afraid to do it, but once they come out from their shells they can do it. It cures an inferiority complex very fast.

What is guilt? For how long a guilt remains! The feeling of guilt is a good hideout for people who have an inferiority complex. They tell themselves that they feel too guilty to be with others, and by this pretext they separate themselves and enjoy their pain. This becomes a pattern of their life, which, in its advanced stage, makes them a cripple for society.

The same kind of people also use Yoga as a hideout. They live separately and think they are doing Yoga, but in fact they don't do Yoga, they simply sit in a corner where no one can see them. Forget about your past and guilt feelings. Your guilt is all created by your mind, and your mind can wipe out this feeling. There is no Mantra, drug, or posture that can cure it. You have to break the pattern by yourself.

By talking you can not heal yourself. You will go on talking, making everything painful. It will never end. You have to break the pattern. Play physical games. Sing and dance.

From a letter

How does one get to feel more confident, to accept oneself more?
We don't accept ourselves when we play the game of others. When we play our own game then we develop confidence. I mean when we stand on our own feet.

What is a way to overcome pridefulness?
If you can beg food from your enemy.

And if you can't?
Too proud.

Where does loneliness come from?
Loneliness comes when a person can't be his own friend. We try to find others from outside to take the place of a friend. For some time we may enjoy their company but again loneliness overpowers the mind.

The feeling of loneliness is the outcome of some hidden desire which can temporarily be fulfilled by association with certain people. But these desires can't be satisfied for long. They come again. Strive to enjoy loneliness. It will help in Yoga. A prisoner who doesn't care about being released is able to enjoy prison.

Is loneliness inside of oneself? Does it follow you?
It is a good thing. It is vairag.

Sometimes the meaninglessness of everything is the cause of sadness. How do you deal with it?
Develop it. It is a dispassionate state of mind which is very important in yogic life.

How?
Sadness when developed can make the consciousness very high; but don't develop sadness to attain friends or the world; that will bring pain.

How do you deal with this sadness — the feeling that you have gone nowhere without any cause?
Accept the meaninglessness of the world and it will push your consciousness to a higher level.

What is sadness and what is happiness? Shouldn't you see God in everything?
To be able to see God in everybody and everything is a very high stage. The main thing is to understand the cause of sadness. Is it a desire for something or for not having anything?

Not to have anything?
That is vairag. In Samadhi a yogi gets vairag, and if coming out of Samadhi he is still attached to the world then it wasn't Samadhi; it was no better than a sleep.

We live in the imagination of others. When we see a person, we don't see the reality of that person — we see only our desires projected onto that person, which is our imagination. In this way we all live in the imagination of others, as long as we don't see the truth.

133

Loneliness in its extreme gives a sense of death, because death is the only thing which can't be shared with others.

*You ask, "What is fear? What is anger? What is pain?" The
root of fear, anger, and pain is ignorance, and ignorance is to
accept the world as true. A person who dreams that a snake
is chasing him runs and cries due to fear. But when he wakes
up he doesn't cry because he knows the dream was not true.
But the dream was true as long as he was asleep.*

The world is as true as a dream; when awakened both are
untrue.

*One can only be free from these devils — fear, anger, pain —
by living in this world unattached, desireless. It's difficult,
but living in the world is not easy either. If both are difficult,
then why should we not try to unwind from the trap, rather
than to wind it more tightly?*

*The worldly traps are grosser traps and can be avoided by
different methods, but the traps of the world inside the mind
are very subtle.*

*A bird trapper ties a revolving bar on a long bamboo pole and
pushes it up in a tree near a bird. When the bird sits on it, the
bar rolls over and the bird hangs upside down. The bird clings
to the roller more tightly due to his fear. Meanwhile the
trapper brings the pole down and captures the bird. Even
after sitting on the roller the bird was still free to fly away,
but it was not really free because in its mind there was no
freedom.*

From a letter

*Even in taming an animal we use love. Anger and violence
never work to win the heart of any creature. Attachment is
not bad if it is used to live together. When we are in a society,
or in a family, we need attachment, ego, desires — but within
a limit. Detachment should be realized in the mind, and not
by throwing away things, not talking, or not relating to
people.*

*The past is dead. Forget it. The future is uncertain, so don't
think on it. The present can be blissful if you accept it as
God's will.*

Yoga is a method by which a person develops higher consciousness. It gives an ability to understand the reality of the world. When this reality is realized, then a person is released from a self-created prison. 99% of the people are in prisons. They imprison themselves by building walls of desires, attachments, needs, demands, and live in pain for their whole lives. Faith and devotion are the two legs that make us stand and walk on the path.
Be in the world, but not of the world. Be alone among people.

From a letter to a man in prison

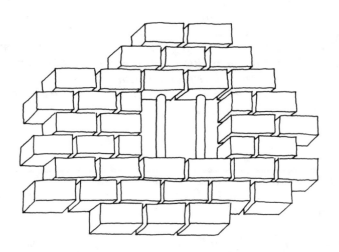

Understanding can only be clear when there is dispassion (non-attachment). If there is desire we will understand desire instead of truth. That is delusion.

By becoming aware of how desire controls our actions, samskaras become thinner and thinner until they are transparent.

How can we see our attachments that interfere with developing dispassion?
You can feel it in all your actions. If a child hides your shoe, you will get upset. You will not say, "I am upset because I am attached to my shoe," but you are.

How can I get rid of attachment?
We are attached because we want to be attached. Without attachment we can't enjoy the world. As long as we want to get pleasure from the world, attachment is needed.

What can I replace my attachments with?
Attachment to God.

How?
You have to experience God to get attached.

As soon as you are aware of your attachments they become like a TV show. You can see the whole drama in your head.

How do you feel about acts of discriminative wisdom which leave a man at a distance from his fellow men?
As long as this distance is there, it is not real discriminative wisdom. You are associating discriminative wisdom with the gross world; it is beyond that. It comes when a person gets dispassion from the world. Ramakrishna Paramahansa, Ramana Maharshi, Chaitanya Mahaprabhu, Buddha, Krishna, Rama — and all incarnations of other religions — they took birth, they did their worldly duties, and they lived in society.

Dispassion doesn't mean to separate oneself from people but to understand that this world is not real. Dispassion is attachment to God.

When a yogi gets dispassion, he sometimes gets the thought to leave the body. But to leave the body by being in the body is real dispassion.

Dispassion is a state of mind in which one can live in desires without desire.

Can one become dispassionate by desiring it?
Sometimes a person can get extreme dispassion by his samskaras or by the grace of God, and then within seconds the chain of attachment breaks. It happens to one person out of millions. But others can also get dispassion by regular practice of Yoga. There is no time limit for this attainment. It depends upon truthfulness in Yoga practices, faith, devotion, and the strong will of an aspirant.

I understand emotion is important on the Bhakti path, but can you have dispassion with emotion?
Dispassion is not a lack of emotion, but a lack of attachment. What is love?

You say, truth, or reality, or God.
Do you think that a man who has dispassion has no love?

Yes. I thought that was why yogis are celibate.
Dispassion tells us that the world is an illusion and not truth. Yogis love God and nature. They try to increase love, and not worldly attachments. Being celibate doesn't mean they hate others.

Desirelessness doesn't mean to become like a rock — without love, without emotions, without doing your natural duties. It's only a stage in which we don't feel that "I am this, I am that," but outwardly everything goes on in the same manner.

Desire creates more desire, and the whole world is created in this way. The silkworm makes a net to imprison himself. In the same way a being makes a net around himself of his attachments, desire, possessiveness, and he sits inside that net in pain and depression. As long as this net is not broken the silkworm remains dormant, but as soon as it is broken the silkworm comes out in the new form of a butterfly, which can fly and make everyone happy.

Desirelessness is Bliss

One who doesn't desire anything owns everything.

YOGA

Faith and devotion are two legs which can make us stand and walk on the spiritual path.

A tree is inside a seed in a subtle form. When the seed is sown the tree comes out in its gross form. In the same way all knowledge is already in our mind and by doing Yoga this knowledge comes out like the tree. Yoga itself is a craziness. We do it only from faith — by hearing about it from others or by reading books. We really don't know what is happening or what will happen. It is like making a building in space. In Yoga we strive from nothing to nothing. First we make a belief in the existence of God, but this belief is mixed with doubts. Then we make it stronger by faith, and we feed it with devotion. Then comes action, which is Atma Vichara *(Self-inquiry). To do this whole process we start from the Gross Body with the practices of* Yama *and* Niyama, Asana, *and* Pranayama. *Next we get a consciousness of the Subtle Body and start the practices of* Pratyahara, Dharana, Dhyana, *and* Samadhi.* *Then we merge into the Causal Body, which is called liberation.*

Faith, devotion, and right thinking are the foundation of spirituality; contentment, compassion, and tolerance are the walls. One who has built this room for himself is safe and in peace . . . God is already with him.

---

*These are the eight steps of Ashtanga Yoga: 1) Yama, observances; 2) Niyama, restraints; 3) Asanas, postures; 4) Pranayama, breath control; 5) Pratyahara, mind control; 6) Dharana, concentration; 7) Dhyana, meditation; 8) Samadhi, superconsciousness.

To achieve benefits in Yoga must one have faith?
*Through Yoga the spiritual benefit, faith, will be developed.
Yoga also gives physical benefits. Aim is most important. The
greatest benefit is obtained from Yoga if it is performed for
the sake of Self realization. There are four states of mind out
of which a person starts Yoga:*
1) Pain
2) Desire for wealth and power
3) Desire to know God
4) Being born with dispassion
*Of all these the first is most common. Even Buddha turned
toward Self realization due to pain.*

What is the object of faith?
Faith can make God real.

Is faith also an illusion?
It is an illusion until it is real.

Is grace also an illusion?
*Ramakrishna Paramahansa had faith in the bronze figure of
Kali, and he received her grace. Actually the power was inside
of him. You can prove it for yourself. When you meditate on
an object very deeply you can realize this. The object is
outside — concentrate on it; your mind will dissolve and the
curtain between inside and outside will disappear. Everything
is in you, and you project it outside. You see what you want
to see. Grace, then, is a helpful illusion, a sattvic illusion.*

What is the quickest way to increase faith?
By disciplining your life pattern.

How would that increase faith?
*When life pattern is disciplined, the mind becomes more
peaceful, and that peace brings faith.*

Love, God, nothingness, can't be taught by words, by correspondence or by reading books. Just like sweetness can't be described. We have to start from faith and build on it until we can experience God. Choose an idea of God and cling to it. The main thing is to be near God.

A baby monkey clings to its mother, but the cat carries her babies in her mouth. These are two stages: first, when you are able to cling, you have to cling to God; when you are beyond the ego of the doer you are like the kitten, surrendered to your helplessness. Then God will carry you.

Do you mean by "disciplined life" to follow some religion?
Religion can't show God, God has no religion. But it's good to follow some order or discipline.

Does it matter which order one follows?
I don't know. Some like cookies, some toast, some tea. Be alone among people. Live in desires without desire. It has no technique, only understanding.

How can we develop devotion?
By developing faith. It's in your hands to dance or sit. If you feel like dancing then dance. If your aim is firm everything is Yoga. In dancing you'll dance for God, in working you'll work for God, and in meditating you'll meditate for God.

What role does devotion play in sadhana?
Faith, devotion, and right thinking are three pillars of spiritual life. Devotion is the light of love. When it grows in a person it spreads out. It goes so deep that you can't say God and love are two different things.

In people's minds, devotion and worship are the same. Is there a difference?
Worship is the active part of devotion. You do something. Devotion itself is a feeling of love toward God. If you do anything or not, still it is there.

Does faith transcend or invalidate the intellect?
When there is faith you don't need discrimination (intellect). You have accepted and you don't have any questions left. But you have to attain this faith. It never comes all at once. In the beginning faith and intellect work in harmony.

What is Atma Vichara?
Atma Vichara, "Who am I," is a very important question in

*Yoga sadhana. It opens the mind and tells you why you are
doing Yoga. Otherwise Yoga can become a mechanical process.
Atma Vichara with Yoga sadhana awakens the consciousness
very quickly, but it needs truthfulness in your own mind. It
is a solitary path. The way of Atma Vichara is so narrow that
two can't be together there. It's not like* Bhakti Yoga. *The
path of Bhakti Yoga is very wide; several can go together.
The end of both paths is God.*

What is the answer to the question, "Who am I?"
*For this we have to search. On the gross level the answer is
different for individual people, but in the end it is one. First
we search on a low level − body, friends, surroundings,
world − and then we see, "I am not that." In this way the
search goes on and on. When the consciousness reaches the
mental sheath it shows us a partial answer, which is not yet
perfect. We understand a little, and that little again is
different for each person. But when the answer comes from
beyond the mental sheath, from the superconsciousness, then
that is the perfect answer, and it is the same for everyone.*

*Atma Vichara, "Who am I," begins in illusion because an
aspirant can't understand the subtlety of "I." But when his
consciousness becomes clearer by Yoga sadhana, then he can
do the real Atma Vichara. Self inquiry starts with words. The
mind talks to itself: "I am not this, I am not this," and so on.
But after regular practice it doesn't talk, it experiences "I
am not this, I am not this." This experience is the real Self
inquiry.*

147

 # ASHTANGA YOGA

What is the way Ashtanga Yoga views the world?
The Self is God and the world is a projection of your mind.

If a person is observing Yama and Niyama* (precepts of right living) in a perfect way, he doesn't need any sadhana. He is perfect in himself. But it's not so easy. As long as the consciousness is on a low level, Yama and Niyama are also on a low level. Yoga and Yama/Niyama reinforce each other. By observing Yama/Niyama one can devlelop the ability to do Yoga, and by doing Yoga one attains higher consciousness.

---

*Yama consists of five parts: Ahimsa, non-violence; Satya, veracity; Asteya, non-stealing; Brahmacharya, sexual continence; Aparigraha, non-hoarding.

Niyama consists of five parts: Shaucha, cleanliness; Santosha, contentment; Tapas, austerity; Svadhyaya, study; Ishvara-pranidhana, surrender to God.

*If you go deeply into one of the five parts of Yama, you will
see that it covers all the other four parts. It is the same way
with Niyamas. Suppose you take* Satya, *"truthfulness,"
it covers* Ahimsa *(non-violence),* Asteya *(non-stealing),
Brahmacharya (continence), Aparigraha (non-hoarding). One
can't be completely truthful unless he observes the other four
parts of Yama. Then finally everything, Yama and Niyama,
dissolves into total surrender to God,* Ishvara Pranidhana, *the
final Niyama.*

Is doing Asanas the same as doing physical exercises —
pushups, running, etc.?

*Asana is not merely a physical exercise. It's a trinity of mind,
breath, and body movement. In physical exercise we work
like a machine to develop muscles and muscular strength. In
Asanas the mind remains aware of movement, or it
concentrates on certain points on the body. Each movement
has its inhalation and exhalation pattern of breath. The
slower the movement, the more mind, body, and breath will
be in tune. In this way Asana makes a perfect Yoga. It is a
meditation. Asanas do not build a huge muscular body, but
they develop the glands which control the growth, actions,
and decay of the body. So by doing Asanas one can
overcome physical weakness and maintain good health.
Asanas give enormous physical and mental strength.*

What is Pranayama and its purpose?

*Pranayama is breath control. It is not simply inhalation and
exhalation. There is awareness of inhalation and exhalation,
which means breath and mind are working together.
Otherwise it would be easy to hike one mile each day and
fulfill the need of Pranayama. The purpose of Pranayama is
to make the breath shallow. When the breath is shallow, the
mind becomes still.*

149

If you keep a lighted candle in a place where the wind is blowing you will see that the flame flickers all the time. The same thing happens inside the body. The breath is like a fan and Chit (mind) is like the candle flame. When we breathe heavily our Chit flickers more, and if the breath becomes shallower the Chit automatically gets still and peaceful. In Samadhi the breath stops. It means the Chit has no vrittis (thought waves). In Pranayama we practice deep breathing, holding, and complete exhalation. By deep breathing we can hold breath for a longer time. When we hold it for a longer time we make more pranic energy and less breath is exhaled. Regular practice of Pranayama brings a time when we inhale, hold, and do not exhale. This stage is called Samadhi. This is one of the methods of reaching Samadhi. There are thousands of methods.

I worry about suffocating when the breath stops.
*When breath becomes shorter through Pranayama, it also
becomes very smooth; there is no pressure at all. There is no
suffocation in Samadhi, this is a misconception.*

*If a person increases Pranayama little by little it is very
effective, but if he does too much one day and stops for ten
days then it is very harmful. It can diminish digestion and
upset the entire system.*

*As the lion, elephant, or tiger is tamed gradually, even so
should prana be brought under control. Otherwise it will kill
the practitioner.*

What is Pratyahara?
*Withdrawing the mind from objects which attract the senses
is Pratyahara. When the senses are dissolved into the mind,
then the next three stages of Yoga can begin — Dharana,
concentration; Dhyana, meditation; Samadhi,
superconsciousness.*

*In the beginning when we practice Pratyahara (withdrawing
the mind from outside objects) we have to protect ourselves
from the object in order to save ourselves from creating a
desire to have it. This is called tapas. In short, giving up
desires is called tapas. But when we master Pratyahara, then
we can live in desires without desire. It means we live in a
society, observing all social rules, but our mind is not
attached to it. Our balance becomes so perfect that we can
move in society without thought of balancing. As long as the
mind is not free from vrittis one can't see what one really is.
Inner silence (stopping of vrittis) is the only way by which
we can see the real Self.*

*The purpose of tapas is to detach the mind from the body; to
watch yourself is the hardest tapas.*

A person learns to ride a bicycle. In the beginning he fixes his eyes on the road, keeps the steering handle straight and firm, turns the pedals smoothly, and tries to keep his balance. He has to think of many things at one time. But once he learns, he does the same things without thinking about balancing, pedaling, steering — everything becomes automatic.

What does Babaji feel about tapas?
Reducing desires is called tapas — not hanging upside down.

*To observe Yama and Niyama is the only true tapas. To sit
on thorns, to sleep on dirt, to live naked, etc., is tapas only
on a gross physical level.*

*Tapas is not a penance, it's a mental training to develop will
power. There are thousands of kinds of tapas. According to
the mental level of an aspirant, one is given a particular kind
of tapas which helps him to train his mind.*

Can you say something about losing body consciousness?
*In deep concentration a person loses awareness of the outside
and also of his body, just as a chess player is ignorant of
outside things while he plays.*

*When Dharana, Dhyana, and Samadhi are all practiced
together, it is called* samyama. *It depends entirely on the
practice of an aspirant to get to the stage of samyama. It
becomes so automatic that as soon as the aspirant sits in
meditation his consciousness begins to shift from Dharana to
Dhyana to Samadhi very swiftly.*

*When the mind is drawn in from the outer world (Pratyahara)
for twelve seconds the state is called Dharana. When Dharana
continues for twelve times twelve seconds (two minutes,
twenty-four seconds) Dhyana begins. When Dhyana
continues for twelve times twelve times twelve seconds
(twenty-eight minutes, forty-eight seconds) it is called lower
Samadhi (Samprajnata Samadhi).*

What is Samadhi?
*An extremely dispassionate state of mind is called Samadhi.
The mind doesn't accept any thoughts or ideas of present,
past, or future. In that stage the mind totally disappears and
is replaced by a superconsciousness, God.*

*After the first Samadhi one sees the illusory nature of
objects. Even in meditation you can begin to feel it. In
Samadhi the world is different. You see an object, but you*

153

will see it differently. Samadhi brings dispassion, or, extreme dispassion is Samadhi.

Extreme desirelessness is Samadhi. When this Samadhi becomes more dense the physical body also disappears. It means we are keeping our body by desire.

As soon as attachment to thoughts is given up, Samadhi is attained. By reinforcing each other, thoughts, senses, and mind smother the whole world. But when one is stopped, the other two stop by themselves. For this we do Yoga.

Yoga sadhana is for stopping unnecessary thoughts. There are two methods to control thoughts: either control thoughts by your will power, or control them by doing Pranayama regularly, which creates a situation where thought stops by itself. Don't try to fight with your thoughts; they will become more furious. First make yourself strong by doing regular sadhana.

When the mind is stopped, the world is stopped.

What is meditation and is it necessary for enlightenment?
It is to drop out all confusion of thoughts. It is important to get out of the pain of our own illusion. What is enlightenment?

I don't know.
Then meditation is necessary.

When the body works, the mind gets rest; and when the body rests, the mind becomes more active. This is the reason why when a person wants to meditate his mind creates more thoughts, strange thoughts . . . unbelievable thoughts, and he becomes upset and stops meditation. This stage remains for six to twelve months. After that the mind wants to reject those thoughts if a person is sincerely trying to meditate.

When I meditate my mind is quiet at first. After a while I begin to daydream. How can I get through this?
It's the pull of the world. You can go deeper and deeper but as soon as you think, "That's it!" you're standing on the earth again. For a long time this happens and then gradually the mind gets unattached to the world and daydreaming stops.

There is no peace in the world. If there is any peace it is only in meditation. At first everyone does false meditation; while one sits different kinds of thoughts come. But this fake meditation turns into true meditation by regular practice. One should not be afraid of the thoughts, but try to eliminate them slowly.

A cotton thread can cut an iron bar if passed over it daily. If you work on Yoga, Yoga will work on you.

Many teachers have been brought here in the past ten years with many methods of meditation. What method do you have for meditation?

The meditator is Ajna, the chakra in the forehead. In any technique you use, the meditator will not change; so if the meditation is done on Ajna it's more direct. If you meditate on a rock or on something else, it is still Ajna meditating. If the rock is not in Ajna, you cannot see it. Anything you see or feel is the function of Ajna. It is the seat of Manas, one of the four minds.

The different methods of meditation are just for tricking the mind out of its normal activity into a state of quiet.

We have to trick the mind by various methods to prevent it from forming thoughts. You will learn by your own higher stage of consciousness.

When I concentrate on Ajna I seem to see a blue spot hovering in space outside of my head.

The dot of blue color you see in Ajna Chakra is the center, or bindu. Sometimes concentration on this makes it disappear, but regular practice of concentration will make it appear and stay. Then go deep inside it; you will see light, very bright light. Although we say the location of Ajna Chakra is behind the eyebrows, it is very subtle. It exists in a form of light and energy, which can be felt. The blue spot you were seeing outside your head was also right: in concentration the blue spot sometimes appears outside, which is the projection of the blue spot inside. Concentrate very deeply on the blue spot, inside or outside, and it will give you peace and bliss.

Can you suggest specific methods for improving concentration in meditation?

Watching the breath is a very good method for developing concentration. It can be practiced all of the time. After a while one can develop awareness of breath even in sleep. If you watch it carefully you will notice that you first inhale, and when you have a full breath there is a short pause; then you exhale, and the breath stops for a short time. If you make a deliberate effort to stop it at the top of the inhale, the method is more effective. The breath should be regular and without sound. Yogis say that one should breathe as one would squeeze a lemon, slowly and firmly.

Is it good to do Mantra and concentrate on Ajna at the same time?

That is the method of Mantra Yoga — the trinity of mind, breath, and sound united at Ajna.

What is the difference between Mantra and Japa?

Mantra is the repetition of sounds or words which have power due to the vibration of the sound itself. Japa is the rhythmic repetition of a name of God. It consists of automatic Pranayama, concentration, and meditation. The main idea in doing Japa is to make the mind thoughtless. Then automatically body consciousness disappears. If your body consciousness disappears, it means your sadhana is going well. The body is the medium of sadhana and the body is the hindrance in sadhana. Japa is a formal method of worshipping God. It should be done privately and preferably with a mala, *or rosary.*

Ajapa, *without repetition of God's name, is a method of tuning mind, Mantra, and breath that can be practiced anywhere at any time, even in sleep.*

In Ajapa Pranayama there is no retention of breath. Inhalation and exhalation should be natural, with the mind fixed on HUM-SAH. HUM is the energy of Shiva, and SAH is the energy of Shakti, so the two sounds encompass God and all of creation. By doing HUM-SAH continually the breath becomes shallow. For practicing Ajapa one takes a deep breath and then exhales, making the exhalation twice as long as the inhalation. After doing this for a few times one can breathe in a natural way, inhaling on HUM and exhaling on SAH. In exhalation the sound of SAH can be prolonged by saying SAH-SAH-SAH. HUM-SAH HUM-SAH HUM-SAH, HUM-SAH when it is repeated often enough it becomes SAH-HUM, with SAH on the inhale and HUM on the exhale. In Sanskrit there are rules of elision called Samdhi. When the sound of visarga (aspirate, in this case the "H" at the end of SAH) comes before a consonant it changes into an "o" sound. So SAH-HUM becomes SO-HUM. SO-HUM SO-HUM SO-HUM SO-HUM, when it is repeated enough "S" and "H" drop and all that remains is OUM or OM. This Mantra works on the different levels of all the bodies: HUM-SAH is the Gross level; SO-HUM, the Subtle level; OM, the Causal level. It all happens by itself when an aspirant regularly practices Ajapa.

Why do you say one should meditate alone?

If a person goes to a place where people are quarreling, he feels anger even if he is not involved in the quarrel. The reason for this is that his mind gets the vibration of anger from others. During concentration, when the mind is free from vrittis, it draws in worldly vrittis, just like a vacuum bottle sucks air when the cork gets loose. If concentration is very deep, then one can't receive vrittis from the outside, but as soon as the concentration weakens the mind fills with several vrittis. Then the aspirant is unable to draw in his mind again, at least for some time.

Is it possible to use ego as a channel?

Without the ego you can't step forward. Ego is action. Without action you can't do anything. When you say, "I have to meditate," this is all action — ego.

So the idea is to purify ego?

Ego gets thinner and thinner, like a black cloud becomes a white cloud, and then the white cloud thins to a fine mist, and through that mist you can see. It doesn't obstruct your vision.

What about ego getting in the way of sadhana?

What ego?

Oh, saying, "Far out!" when I have a good meditation.

It's OK. Don't worry about ego, just meditate.

Is meditation helpful to everyone?

If you really meditate. If the mind goes to the bakery to purchase bread while you meditate, it can't help. Try to stop the mind for five minutes, then you will feel bliss. Meditation is a result of sadhana. If your practice goes well then meditation will come by itself. The mind starts going inward without any effort. No one can teach meditation, it is an

159

action inside your mind and only you can know what you are doing. If I say concentrate on Ajna you can't understand what I mean by my words, and I can't see what you are doing. But if what I say has some meaning for you and you do it, you will get it. If a person reads one hundred books on Yoga, can he concentrate better? The main thing is to practice.

A man once did sadhana in a jungle cave. God gave him darshan and asked, "What would you like?"
"That whatever I think will come true," he replied.
"All right. Anything you think will be true."
The man became very happy, he thought of good food, and the food was there. He thought about a nice bed, and the bed was there. All of a sudden he thought, "What will happen if this cave falls down?" As soon as he thought this, the cave fell down.
He got power, but he had no control over his mind because his sadhana was not deep enough. We need to do sadhana so that we will become able to control our thoughts.

Although there are millions of methods of Yoga, the aim is one and that is to make the mind free from thought waves. For this, meditation is the most important thing. But it's not easy to meditate because of obstacles that come in the way. The main obstacles are two: first, the physical body weakness, illness, stiffness, and so on. Second, samskaras (impressions of actions of past births). The physical hindrances can be cured by doing Asanas every day and by taking a sattvic diet. But the obstacles due to samskaras are very strong. An aspirant is drawn to the wrong path, and even though he knows that he is going the wrong way, he can't stop himself. Gambling, drug addiction, thoughts of hurting others, all the passions are impurities of the mind. The mind is purified in two ways, either by doing Pranayama and meditation, or by cultivating positive qualities. For developing positive qualities, selfless action, satsang (the company of spiritual people), study of scriptures, and reading life histories of saints are important.

To do regular Yoga sadhana is difficult. Very few people can do it. When Asana, Pranayama, and Mudra *are practiced regularly for three or four years then one gets the ability of concentration, meditation, and Samadhi, which is called samyama. As soon as a yogi has the ability of samyama, his Yoga becomes perfect. Another way is the Zen method, which is called* Dhyana Yoga, *or Ch'an in Chinese. Through this system the mind is trained to do samyama directly. In earlier times the head of a Zen monastery would admit only students who were able to start at this stage. Ashtanga Yoga, however, is for everybody. A stone mason uses rocks of all kinds; he uses them to make walls according to their shapes and sizes. In the same way Ashtanga Yoga gives shape to all kinds of students for the masonry of Yoga. After receiving a shape, some go to* Dhyana Yoga, *some to* Laya Yoga, *some to* Nada Yoga, *some to* Kundalini Yoga, *some to* Bhakti Yoga, *and so on.*

Is Zen enlightenment different from that of other paths?
Realization of truth is enlightenment. Truth can't be different for Buddhists, Hindus, Christians, or others. For me all sadhanas are the same if they are practiced for realization of God.

Are religions, particularly Christian religions, the same as Yoga? Will reading the Bible, going to church, and so forth, bring the same results?
Religion and Yoga are two different things. Religion teaches how to live in the world, Yoga teaches how to get out of the world. Yoga isn't owned by any religion.

Which way do you advise people to follow — Karma Yoga or Bhakti Yoga?
Both are important for the spiritual path.

Doesn't Bhakti Yoga encourage a feeling of dualism? How can we be one with God?
Bhakti Yoga can't be practiced without dualism, lover and beloved. In Bhakti Yoga an aspirant relates to God with different attitudes such as being a servant, a friend, a wife, a lover, or a parent of God. In higher stages the dualism remains only in the names, like the sun and its rays, the ocean and the waves, which are not separate.

I've had initiation into 'Shabda'. Can you discuss its relationship to Ashtanga Yoga?
When the body and mind are purified by regular Pranayama and Shath Karma*, *or by meditation, then a kind of sound which already exists inside the body becomes louder and can be heard by the ear. The sound changes into light in its*

---

*Shath Karma consists of six practices for cleansing the inner as well as the outer body.

advanced stage. It can be heard by deep concentration on Ajna or Anahata Chakra. It is called Nada Yoga or Surat Shabda Yoga.

The inner sound, Nada, can be that of a flute, bells, sitar — there are nine different sounds. When Nada appears it shows that the Nadis (subtle nerve channels) are purified. If the mind is concentrated on that sound, the sound changes in various ways. In this way the Chit dissolves into Nada and Samadhi is attained. Actually this sound is a vibration of the Nadis which we can feel inside our head and heart, but the learning process is by the ears so we feel it by the ears. The sound should appear in the right ear and we should concentrate there. After some months' practice the sound switches to the top of the head, and then we have to concentrate on that spot.

By deep concentration on the Nada you can hear its subtlest form which is the echo of that Nada. For changing the sound you have to use will power. Sometimes you can become attached to hearing a certain sound, then you have to make the effort to change it to one of the other sounds. By being alone in caves, or on beaches, or in jungles a yogi develops emotion. This emotion creates Nada. Nada is a purified state of mind. The more pure the mind, the clearer the Nada will become. When Nada comes in its subtle form it creates Samadhi.

Dualism is more than one and less than two.

I'd like to ask about mandalas (visual symbols). In order to reach desired results, does a person pick a certain mandala and then change it from time to time?
Mandalas are designed for certain energies. A method of worship using Mantras and yantras (mandalas) is Tantra.

If one makes a mandala, his own mandala, is it a good thing to concentrate on?
Concentration is always good. Do it any way you can.

What is the benefit of using mandalas?
Mandala is a tantric language, a way of explaining energy. If you meditate on a mandala with its meaning it can help concentration.

Does every mandala have one meaning?
Each line, circle, triangle, square, color has a meaning.

Are there some that heal?
(Nods yes)

What is the power in Mantra?
Mantra is sound, which activates the energy centers. In the beginning there was a sound — no earth, nor life. That sound made a form of bindu, a point of energy; then it split in two and assumed a form like the figure eight. This started consciousness plus energy and was the beginning of creation. In the beginning there was nothing but bliss, but then creative energy overpowered it, and the whole universe took form. Eventually ignorance overpowered creative energy, and desires and attachments were born to sustain the world.

Why don't you speak?
One reason is to avoid quarrels. (Laughter) The second is because talking causes loss of energy. Energy is lost primarily in two ways — by sex and by sound. The origin of both

sound and sex is the same place, Muladhara Chakra at the base of the spine. When we talk we do so by exhalation, and we lose tremendous energy this way. This energy can be felt if you stop talking for a few days and then start talking again. By not using sound we preserve energy which can be used for meditation.

Are Mantras and kirtan (spiritual singing) OK while in mauna (silence)?
If you can do complete silence that is better. If you do Mantra and kirtan while in mauna that is OK.

What is silence?
Thoughtlessness. Silencing the mind is real silence. To stop talking is one way to begin to silence the mind.

Silence is an austerity. You control your desire to talk. By talking, people try to impress others and attract others, which you can't do if you are in silence. In silence you have to develop tolerance. At first it is difficult to do because you separate yourself from others by not expressing yourself. But gradually the mind reduces that ego and an aspirant accepts the situation, which develops tolerance and reduces anger.

I have a real yearning to be silent for a while, but I have a family and a job and don't know how to do it.
I have a larger family (indicating the satsang). You can do it when you get time.

I guess I am embarrassed to do it in public. It is easy to do when I want to.
Anything is easy when you want to do it.

165

What are our dreams?
Our actions of present, past, and far past are in the subconscious. When the physical body rests these impressions rotate, and they feel real to our senses.

What are dreams rotating around?
The mind is always active, even in our sleep. All impressions rotate in the mind. If you watch dreams you find they make a strange story; some parts come from different events in the present and past, and some come from past lives. One who learns to watch dreams can read the past and see the future.

Dream is a function of the Subtle Body. Yoga distinguishes three "normal" conditions of the consciousness and one supernormal. The normal conditions are Jagrat, *waking;* Svapna, *sleep with dreaming;* Sushupti, *deep sleep. The supernormal state is* Turiya, *or deep Samadhi. There is an enormous difference between the unconsciousness of deep sleep and the trance of Turiya. In deep sleep one has no will, no knowledge, it is essentially a restorative state for the physical body. In Turiya the yogi is completely lucid, extremely aware, and enjoys the subtle knowledge of truth. When the Gross Body is fatigued, Tamas Guna overpowers Rajas Guna and makes the body incapable of action. The muscles relax and the body grows heavy and inert. It sleeps. At this time the Subtle Body takes over; it recollects the actions and relationships engaged in by the Gross Body and produces visions of these actions in the mind. Usually there is no mental control over dreams. The pictures flow in a confusing and disorderly fashion, taking the path of least resistance, because the Intellect (discriminating power and Rajas predominant) has been overpowered by Tamas Guna. The Subtle Body is sometimes referred to as the Astral Body. Due to the life force of prana, the Subtle Body exists beyond the life and death of the Gross Body, and so it has*

166

access to the samskaras (impressions) of past births, the
desires and experiences of pleasure and pain. Through
sadhana a person can learn to control his dreams. By so doing
he may overcome samskaras, the very factor that causes
rebirth. He may achieve partial or even total enlightenment in
dreams by willing to do so. The ability to control one's
dreams removes them from the state of Svapna into the state
of astral projection.

Is spirit-consciousness the same as the Astral Body?
What is spirit? Consciousness is a word used for mind, Self,
God. When we say good and bad spirits, we don't mean
consciousness. Spirit is energy mixed with samskaras. If
samskaras are bad, we say bad spirit. Astral Body is a very
pure form.

What is the difference between astral projections and dreams?
A vast difference. When we dream we cannot control the
dream; if we could it would be astral projection.

What does a dream involve?
We receive a dream by impression; we feel with the five
senses but have no control over them. But there is a method
of Yoga by which one can control dreams.

Are there emotions and ego in astral projection?
Without ego nothing can be projected. Emotions are also
there in their subtle form. When we fly in our astral body and
meet someone, we can feel the pain and emotions of that
person.

I know several people who say astral travel can be helpful on the spiritual path. Is this true?
If they are doing it. They sleep in their sleeping bags until
10:00 and they say they have been astral traveling. After a
month they gain ten pounds of weight. Still they say, "astral

167

travel." Dream, astral travel, and Samadhi are functions of the Subtle Body. When Tamas Guna is predominant we dream, when Rajas Guna is predominant we astral travel, and when Sattva Guna is predominant we are in Samadhi. Dream sadhana is one of the methods to achieve astral travel, or even Samadhi.

Can you get stuck in a place when doing astral travel?
Don't get inside a box! (Laughter)

If we do dream sadhana, does it take the place of regular sadhana?
Dream sadhana can be done in addition to regular sadhana. If you don't do regular sadhana you can't do dream sadhana.

Why do we forget our dreams?
To remember them is a sadhana — to keep them in mind and analyze them. If the dream is Tamas Guna predominant, we forget it.

How do we stop our thoughts at night so that we can sleep deeply?
First stop the thoughts in the day, then you can stop them at night.

Is symbolism in dreams only personal, or are there some universal symbols?
Some of each. Dreams of the Elements are universal. For example, a dream of water means that the Water Element is predominating. It relates to the second chakra. Tamas Guna controls the first and second chakras, Rajas controls the third, and Sattva controls the fourth and fifth chakras.

(Asked by a seven year old boy) Is life a dream or a meditation?
Life is a meditation when you know it is a dream.

What is the discipline?

*Write down your dreams early in the morning every day
for one year. This will develop awareness of dreams. After
six months or a year select the dreams that are linked or have
been repeated several times, and try to dream those dreams
one at a time. This will develop control over dreams. When
you are able to dream what you want to dream, then try to
dream of a place which you have visited. After that is
successful try to dream of a place you have not visited. This
will develop the power of astral traveling. After some practice
you can dream of doing Yoga and meditation. Try to dream
that your Kundalini is awakening and all energy centers are
opening up.*

*It takes concentration to dream what you want to dream. So
before going to bed you should concentrate on the subject
that you want to dream. Meditate for four or five minutes on
the thousand petaled lotus, or on your luminous form, then
bow to God and go to sleep.*

*To dream of the thousand petaled lotus is very good. To
dream of chakras, light, fire, water, wind, and the Elements of
your own body is an indication of purified nerve channels.
Learn to control your dreams.*

Is a dream acting out one's psyche?
Life is a dream. In a dream you dream your dream.

Just as one medicine can't cure all diseases, so one particular Yoga can't help everyone. Each person is unique in nature, body structure, and samskaras; each has his own talents and his own handicaps. Some are born artists, poets, mathematicians, scientists, and a little practice opens the whole field of their knowledge. In the same way some are born liberated. They understand that they are pure Self, separate from all worldly illusions, and they never identify themselves with the body. Some are born without the slightest understanding of God, Self, peace. What they see and feel through their sense organs is reality to them. Yet through Yoga they, too, can develop an understanding that there is something beyond body and mind.

SADHANA

Would you define sadhana as spiritual practice?
*Sadhana is to get perfection. What is perfection? Perfection
for each person is different. You draw a line and it is perfect
for you, but an artist doesn't see it perfect. He draws another
line and sees it perfect. A person with a magnifying glass
comes and sees the line thick and thin and says it is not
perfect. The edge of a sword is so perfect, and no one can
deny it, but if you see the edge under a microscope you will
see that it is like a chain of mountains. Perfection differs
according to its subtlety.*

What's the point of sadhana?
To get out of the illusion of the world is the point of sadhana.

*We have to live in this world. The world is full of pain — even
the pleasure of the world is pain. But we have to go through
this pain to get bliss. Bliss is freedom from thoughts, and the
world is a bundle of thoughts. By regular Yoga practice, faith
and devotion, and by cultivating good qualities we can attain
that blissful stage. No one can give this stage to anybody. We
all have to attain it by ourselves.*
There are four doors to salvation:

Satsanga, *association with the truth through meeting with
spiritual people and reading spiritual books.*
Vichara, *Self inquiry, asking "Who am I?"*
Santosha, *contentment in any situation, whether we gain
or lose.*
Samta, *equality. All are equal, from an insect to a saint,
because Atman in every being is the same and God lives
in every being in the form of Atman.*

171

One door is enough to get in the house. When you are in the house all doors unite there.

When you are in Yoga all your actions become Yoga, because you are aware of your actions. When you are aware of your actions you can't forget God. God is so vast that there is no limit, and a jiva, who is so small, can meet God from any direction, but still can't reach the limit. So the method of obtaining an unlimited God is also unlimited. Those who say, "This is the only way (or religion) to obtain God," are in illusion.

A path to God that disclaims, other valid paths or methods is ignorance. Sometimes, when a person makes an idea of God and worships it with devotion, he develops a kind of fanatic feeling which creates different kinds of illusions such as disclaiming other paths, religions, sects.

We give name and form to understand God in illusion. It helps in developing faith and devotion. But if a person says that a certain form of God is the only God, then he is in illusion within illusion. For development of his own faith he can believe that his understanding of God is the sole and supreme form, but he can't force others to accept his way. It is like a child who thinks that his father is the strongest man in the world. For him it is true, but it is not true for everyone.

Will we know our path when we start on it?
When you are determined to find it the right path comes from inside. First thing is firm determination. No one can learn from others if he has no ability to learn. What we are learning is already inside of us; we are not getting it from outside.

172

A person who hasn't a musical ear can't pick up music from hearing other people play. I don't mean that a teacher is not necessary but that the quality of learning is within the student. Truth is beyond this. You can't see truth in a teacher while you are still in illusion. You have to go beyond this, and that you can do by yourself. Then there is no "you and I." "You and I" are only an illusion.

What is a guru and his purpose?
A guru is one who has wisdom and is capable of teaching. The parents are the first guru. The child goes to school, and his teachers there are the second guru. Then he desires to attain peace and he seeks a person who can tell him a way to find it. That is the spiritual guru. Above all these is the real guru, which is your own true Self. All gurus are merged in that guru. One who is established in the real Self doesn't need a physical guru.

A guru can only point towards a tree and say, "Look, there is a bird sitting on a branch." His duty is finished and the student's duty begins. The student tries to see the bird. He moves his head up and down and sideways, and sometimes he asks, "Where is the bird?" The teacher again points his finger and says, "Look straight along my finger." The student finally sees the bird. The act of seeing is within him, but he needs to use his vision in the right manner.

Just as the ground is important for growing a seed, in the same way faith is the ground for Yoga's growth. Faith is the real teacher, faith is the real Yoga, and faith is the real attainment. We project our faith on some person as a teacher and we feel his love, peace, and wisdom inside us. If we don't project our faith on that person we can't feel anything. He will be just another man.

Who can initiate?

Your faith. Initiation has no meaning if you have no faith. Once a guru teaching archery to the Pandava Princes would not let a tribal boy become his student. The boy made a clay statue of the guru, practiced in front of it, and achieved greater success than the other students. It happened because his faith in that statue was so real. If you have faith in a guru, or in the image of a guru, it can give you the ability to finish the ego. Then you can experience God directly.

What reason is there to be around a guru if you have faith in God?

It is not important. When a person realizes that he can attain knowledge by his own sadhana, his own Self becomes guru.

Is there no other way the guru can help when you are around him?

He helps all the time. If you have full faith, then you are not two — you are one.

Do you have a guru in your tradition?

Yes, I have a guru.

Is your guru in his body?

For me, he is always in his body.

Can you communicate with him at will?

Yes, he is in me.

175

Will you explain what devotion to a teacher means?
*Devotion to a teacher is to respect and to love him.
Attachment gets so dense that a person doesn't feel the
difference between God and guru. And truly they are not
different.*

Are you talking about a teacher or a guru?
*I am talking about God or guru. You can say, "This is a good
driving teacher." Your devotion to him is to respect his
driving ability and no more. I'm talking about quite a
different thing, a teacher who is helping others to attain
enlightenment.*

What is the difference?
*Working for food and working for enlightenment are not the
same.*

Should one have attachment for a teacher, for guru, for God?
*Attachment to God is devotion, and devotion is important
for enlightenment. Devotion is not a small thing, it affects
many things.*

**I feel that the desire for and the attachment to a guru is very
harmful and that one can't get beyond it.**
That's true if you are trapped on a physical level.

**How can one recognize a 'Sat Guru' (one who has reached
the truth)?**
*Realized and unrealized yogis are all the same in their bodies,
the difference is in their consciousness. An enlightened man
holds an apple in his hand, but the thought of apple is not in
his mind; while an unenlightened man holds an apple in his
hand and also in his mind. Both can do stupid things, but the
one who has a doer's ego creates samskaras by his actions,
whereas the other remains free.*

Are there any criteria by which one can tell who is a real guru and who is fake? So many are coming to America and the West now that it's hard to discriminate.
If you have faith in a garbage can, it can be your guru. Poison kills and poison cures.

How can one determine if a guru is enlightened, and is it important?
You must have faith to feel the enlightenment. In one sense a guru is an ordinary person; faith brings grace. Without faith you can see an enlightened person and get nothing from him.

Can you, Babaji, recognize enlightened people?
Light never hides.

Can all recognize that light?
Not blind people.

You wrote that if a pickpocket sees a saint he will only see his pockets; what does a saint see?
He sees a saint.

If an enlightened being can see what the future holds, then how is it possible for him to use will in directing the course of his life?
An enlightened being has no separate will from God. He has no ego of being a doer. Anything that happens through him is God's will.

Does an enlightened being repeat the life cycle, "sometimes in a smaller circle and sometimes in a bigger circle?"
It is God's will if he gets another body to be in the world, but he acts like a shadow of God. Shadow has its existence, but that existence depends on the object. If the object is removed the shadow will disappear. The "circle" can be smaller and bigger in the same way.

177

Did you ever see anyone become enlightened through a gesture, a smile, or a touch?
I have seen enlightenment come by the ability of the person, not by the touch. One who is ready to explode will explode anyway.

Some teachers say we don't have to do anything, just "Be as you are."
It's a very simple thing to say, but if we really think on it, "Be as you are," then we will find we are not in our real being. Our every action is governed by ego, attachment, desires. If "Be as you are" is something different, a state where there is no ego, attachment, or desires, then we have to work hard to attain that stage.

Yoga doesn't say not to do your social duties. You should do all your duties towards society, but keep your mind in Yoga — like a circus girl who walks the tightrope, takes swings and performs several feats, but always keeps her mind on her balance.
By running away from the world no one can get peace. Anywhere you go the problems will go with you, because the problems are inside you and not outside. The outside is simply a projection of inside.
A human being has a discriminative mind, so he is capable of stopping the pull of bad tendencies. If samskaras, or fate, were the sole master of our lives we would not try to attain the truth. We would leave it in the hands of fate. But we don't do that. We look for food when we're hungry, we defend ourselves when attacked. We know we can't sit like a rock waiting for fate to feed and protect us, to arrange everything for our future. If we know that fate is not our master in day to day life, we should realize we can't wait for fate to lead us to the truth. We should start working to attain the truth.

A person who says, "I don't want to do anything, I just want to be," is deluding himself. He doesn't know himself. How can he say, "I just want to be?" If he means he wants to sit in his ignorance and pain, he will remain sitting forever.

What do we surrender to God?
We surrender our ego. Surrender doesn't mean to become like a rock and not do anything.

In what sense do we surrender to guru?
When we project guru outside, we are really surrendering our ego self to our real Self. But at first we need some reason to do that. A physical guru becomes such a reason.

Is it necessary to meet a guru to become a realized being?
If you find one it can help. Guru is your own real Self. Go inside and you will find.

Then why does he manifest outside?
You are manifesting your world. God manifests God. It's all God, but we made it world. Your own desire is projecting it, and you are capable of finishing it. A being in its natural form is God, and the same being is the world when polluted by ego, desire, and attachment.

How important on a practical level is a guru?
Someone who understands your mental level can tell you which of the many Yoga methods is right for you. Also, it is important to get support from someone whom you accept as higher. A person can cook for you, but he can't eat for you. Even a perfect master can't eat for you. It's good to have faith in a living master, but if you work, you will achieve your aim. It's better to have faith in one's own Self. Without that, faith in a master won't remain long. Guru lies within, not without.

When a teacher is needed is he there?
Yes. Need made the airplane, it will make a teacher; but the need must be real.

Can you have more than one teacher?
It depends on how you feel about a teacher: if it is simply for learning new methods then it is all right. A bee takes honey from several lotuses but never stays on one after sunset, when it closes. She doesn't want to be imprisoned within the lotus for the whole night. She needs honey, but she also needs freedom.

Can we gain freedom without following a master?
All answers are inside us and we have to realize them by ourselves.

The ship is steered by one rudder. The rudder is within the ship, the guru is within you, and that guru is your own Self. The whole world is a teacher and we are learning from everybody. It doesn't mean that one can understand everything at once. Some answers are very deep inside and some are not so deep. The higher the consciousness goes, the deeper the power of understanding goes. We are all different in our samskaras, our thought, and our senses. Because of these differences, each one takes his own meaning out of the sayings of others and acts accordingly.

Can we use the mind to kill the mind, or do we need a perfect master?
We use a thorn to pry out a thorn; we use iron to cut iron. When we do Yoga we use our minds to stop the thought waves. You can say it's using mind to kill the mind.

I feel we need a perfect master to take us the last step to God.
Attain highest consciousness by deep meditation, and this highest consciousness will be the perfect master.

When a person realizes that he can attain knowledge through his own sadhana, his own Self becomes his guru. Everything becomes clear to him step by step.
For sadhana do: Asanas to keep the body fit; Pranayama for purification of the nerve channels and the mind; concentration for one-pointedness. If these three things are practiced regularly, then slowly one achieves higher

181

consciousness. This higher consciousness is the guru. *One who knows this secret remains in the state of cosmic consciousness forever.*

A yogi should select a particular pattern of sadhana and work on it every day. Then he can specialize on that sadhana. All sadhanas are for making the mind free from vrittis, so what's the use of doing one thousand different things? It's not necessary to do all six purification methods, eight Pranayamas, twenty-five Mudras *, and eighty-four Asanas. An aspirant should select things according to his nature, or as his teacher selects for him.

By doing regular sadhana the path of energy going up becomes clearer. Day by day an aspirant gains the ability to understand the difference between truth and illusion.

Can one follow two different paths at once?
One path is enough to reach the destination. To go halfway by one path and then halfway by another path will not bring any progress. But if one path doesn't suit you, then you have to change it.

Can one know reality, or truth?
Truth is beyond senses. All that we experience by our senses is still illusion. But when God shines in the form of Self inside a person, the association of such a person makes a feeling of God, truth, love, which is called satsang.

---

*Mudras are special postures and mental attitudes used to intensify concentration.

You have said that satsang is meeting with people who are seeking God. How can we find God outside with other people? Don't we have to meet Him inside?
What is outside? Outside is a projection of inside. If we are not inside of you, then we are not outside.

Is God here, now?
It is true that God is there where He is worshipped. That's why satsang is very important. One should not just listen to the thoughts and ideas discussed in satsang, we must make those ideas a part of our lives. We have to take on those good qualities — otherwise one will be just like a parrot who can sing Mantras but doesn't get any benefit from them.

Satsang teaches us how to live together and how to love each other. This is the foundation of Yoga and it is the first thing we must learn. Yoga methods are easy to learn, but learning tolerance, compassion, and contentment is difficult. We can't learn by hiding in a cave, we learn by being with people. If you float in love, then all who are around you will float in love. By sadhana one can attain this state.

No one can make heaven on earth until he has made heaven inside of himself first. It is like holding a candle in the dark which is not lit and telling others, "Follow me."

When you are working on the inside, is it proper to work spiritually on the outside as well?
You don't need to work on the outside; your light will spread outside by itself.

Is there a conflict between serving mankind and serving spiritual needs?
Holding nose and holding breath isn't the only way.
Everyday life should be pure and full of good qualities; then there is no conflict. A person who is aware of developing positive qualities is a real yogi. Sainthood is not in dressing in a particular dress, in giving speeches on spirituality. It's in our actions, in our behavior, in our truthfulness. Saints and non-saints are physically the same, but mentally they are different.

Can a person be spiritual without being a member of any spiritual group?
Although a person has no trademark of spirituality, it doesn't mean he is unspiritual. One who is honest, truthful, loving, and ready to help others; one who has less anger, pride, jealousy is already spiritual even though he isn't a disciple of a guru or doesn't belong to a community, sect, or ashram*. Yes, there are several spiritual people without a trademark, and they never classify themselves among spirituals. This egoless spirituality is wonderful.

---

* Ashram is a home, living quarters, for a group of people who have similar spiritual goals.

*Once a blind man was coming from a well at night with a
pitcher of water on his head and a lighted lantern in his hand.
A man met him on the way and said, "How stupid! You are
blind, so why carry a lantern?" The blind man said, "It is for
you, so that you will not knock me down." Our sadhana is a
lantern that lights our way even if we're blind.*

What should I work on the most in my sadhana?
Not to lean on others.

*For a real truth seeker, to live in an ashram for the whole life
is like growing plants under a huge tree. Under the shade of
a big tree the plant first grows, then its growth stops. One
should practice Yoga independently, taking full responsibility
for himself. Group discipline is only to maintain a group.
In Yoga only self discipline is important. An army is very
disciplined, but they don't get enlightenment. When you are
in a group you have to accept the discipline of the group, not
because the discipline will give you enlightenment, but to
make the work of the group easier. In a group doing the same
kind of sadhana, all individuals will not attain the same
results, because each is different in Gross Body, Subtle Body,
and in samskaras. A group or ashram is good only for
learning. When you have learned everything, you have to
practice by yourself.
Living in a community is a different thing. The aim is to
fulfill a desire to live in a joint family. This is a natural desire
in human beings and in certain animals. Because in Western
culture there is no joint family system, the natural desire
comes out in a different way. People want someone to take
charge and tell them what to do and what not to do. It's
not bad, but sadhana is your own thing and not a part of the
commune. Sadhana is a personal thing and not something to
be done collectively. The methods are for achieving purity*

and clarity of mind so as to be able to distinguish between truth and illusion. To watch yourself every moment is Yoga. To attain the ability of watching oneself we practice all the other methods — Asana, Pranayama, meditation.

For how many years does one do a sadhana to get enlightenment?
It depends on the sincerity of one's aim. It can happen in a flash of light, but also it can take years, or even several births.

I've heard it said that a person can become too attached to practice.
We use medicine as long as we're not cured. After that we throw away the bottles. Attachment to practice is important as long as the result is not obtained.

Is it possible after enlightenment to wake and wonder what it's all about?
After enlightenment the past becomes unimportant.

In Yoga sadhana the mind works like a ball: the more you hit it the more it rebounds. So you have to keep on hitting it with regular sadhana.

A farmer had several cows and bulls. He ploughed his fields using a hand plough pulled by his bulls. One day he saw that a young bull was becoming very strong. He patted it on the back and said to himself, "Tomorrow I'll put this young bull on my plough." The farmer went into his house, and the young bull was so happy he began jumping up and down. The other cows and bulls asked him what was the matter. "Tomorrow I'm going to plough," he said, filled with pride. All the younger bulls looked at him with respect as if he were becoming a king, but the old bulls just nodded and went back to their grass. The young bull was so happy that he would go up to everyone he saw and say, "Tomorrow I'm going to plough!" The next morning the farmer took him out to the field and put him under the plough. He was young and strong, so he ran very fast. All day he ran with the plough. By evening he was so exhausted he could hardly walk up to the cow shed. When he reached the shed the younger bulls all ran up to him as if he were a great warrior; and some older bulls came up and asked, "What did you do?" He looked at them and sighed, "I ploughed the whole field!" And then he collapsed on the ground. The older bulls laughed and said, "In the future, go slow, don't run."

I made a story for you, but I did the same thing as you are doing when I was about nineteen years old. I would jump like a new horse all the time, trying different methods of Yoga. But I learned by experience that sadhana should go very smoothly. Some day you will also experience the same thing. If you drop too much butter on a fire all at once it will put out the fire. If you put the butter on little by little it will increase the fire.

Do sadhana according to the time you can spare for it. Don't do too much and don't do too little. The main thing is to avoid the low point where the body and mind develop sloth and laziness and also to avoid the peak point where the body and mind break from pushing too hard.

Yoga is calming and pleasant if you build it up like a building. Do some each day, otherwise it will be a burden and you will run away. A musician works ten to twelve hours a day to learn music. Actually he learns the method in a day, but works on the method for several years.

Those who won the gold medals in the Olympics worked hard, very hard, and some won the medal and some didn't. Learning Yoga is not difficult, but to work on Yoga regularly is very difficult, because there is no immediate gain. This disheartens the yogi at times. But one who works regularly, even though he doesn't win a gold medal, achieves a very high stage of consciousness. There is nothing to lose.

Yoga is an intoxication which makes addiction. Its taste is bitter, but without taking it one can't feel good. For attaining peace regular sadhana is the only medicine. Sometimes sadhana becomes as bitter as quinine, but the patient should take it anyway.

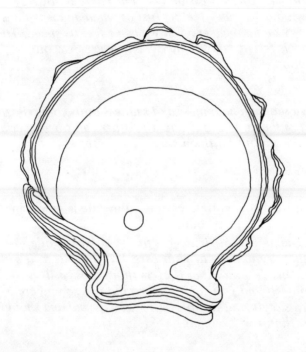

If you want to collect pearls, you have to dive deep. So don't confuse your mind by sitting on the beach and expecting pearls to come sit in your basket.

Regular sadhana works inside the body and mind very slowly. For three or four years we actually don't understand what is happening. After that the mind gets the ability to understand the effect of sadhana. One should not be disheartened by apparent lack of progress in sadhana. There is always progress, but we can't feel it. Just as when an airplane is high in the sky and going very fast we can't feel its speed. The progress is felt at takeoff and when we are near our destination.

In Yoga sadhana happiness and sadness both come. Both are part of sadhana. Without one, the other can't be experienced. But we shouldn't let them stop our practices.

I find it hard to meditate because someone is practicing on drums in the next room.

I understand how difficult it is to do sadhana while someone is beating drums next to your ears. But it is a test. It's also a sadhana inside a sadhana. If everything goes easily you can't test yourself and you can't understand where you are. Go forward slowly and firmly. Every step in sadhana should be firm so that it will not slip.

Would living in a cave help my concentration, help me to get away from all the noise and confusion in my house?

If a person is living in a cave and his mind is attached to the outer world, then he is not in a cave. It's good to do sadhana in a cave for some time, but your cave is inside of you. Why don't you concentrate on Anahata, the heart chakra? It is the emotional mind and will take you to the same place as Ajna. Concentrating on the heart center increases the emotions; if you feel it is better for you, it is not necessary to concentrate on other places.

190

How can one do Yoga when living with people who don't?
*Some people can't do Yoga even when living around those
who do! If a person has vairag (dispassion), he can do Yoga
anywhere. A king can do Yoga and also rule his country.
Yoga trains the mind. By our minds we hear noise, people,
quarrels, and so forth, but if we train the mind to ignore
these things they don't bother us. It depends on our aim. A
man who wants to purchase things sees what is in the store,
but a friend who goes with him for company just smokes
cigarettes and doesn't notice the things in the store.*

*A person works hard to achieve worldly things because he
sees them as real and he believes in them. But very few can
think about the reality of the Self and work hard for it. Of
those who think about it, very few can believe in it. Of those
who believe, very few are free from doubts.*

**I seem to be losing faith. Nothing significant appears to be
happening to me. I keep on expecting some kind of
profoundly moving, absorbing experience or transformation
of my consciousness.**
*As long as the mind is in confusion of thoughts, nothing
happens very fast. But as soon as the thought waves are
stopped, it happens — just as one spark can burn a huge pile
of hay in one second. Regular practice purifies the mind, and
an aspirant automatically adopts good qualities, which
strengthens his faith. There is no medicine or Yoga by which
a person becomes enlightened in a day.*

*In sadhana several good and bad things happen. Sometimes
a yogi gets much faith and sometimes he loses faith. If the
aim is strong he doesn't quit Yoga sadhana, even when he
loses his faith. Yoga sadhana is life. Once you start it, go on*

191

doing Yoga for your whole life, and one day you will see that all actions are Yoga.

If the aim is perfect the chain of sadhana never breaks. Traveling, working, eating, talking, everything becomes sadhana.

Spirituality is not simply doing Asanas, Pranayama, meditation, or singing spiritual songs. Developing good qualities within is spirituality. No one can develop these qualities in one day. An aspirant fights the constant battle within himself to overpower the opposites, good and bad, pleasure and pain. In Hinduism all these things are explained in the form of stories, like the Ramayana *and the* Mahabharata. *The wars in these stories are going on inside every human being all the time in the form of negative or positive qualities. To be aware that you are fighting these battles is sadhana, spiritual practice.*

Sadhana should be part of life. God is within you. Worship Him in the form of love to all beings.

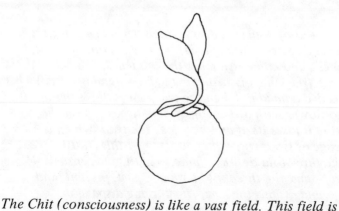

The Chit (consciousness) is like a vast field. This field is ploughed by good deeds and the soil is turned upside down. The insects and weeds which live on the surface are like the bad habits we have developed. They are buried under the ground by the plough of good deeds. The worms which live underground are like our samskaras, tendencies from past births. They are exposed above the soil and are eaten up by birds or are consumed by the heat of the sun.

When this field of Chit is ploughed again and again, the soil breaks. Then it must be irrigated by the practice of Asanas and Pranayamas. The moisture from the irrigation rots the buried weeds and insects, which makes the soil rich. After that the seed of concentration is sown on that ground, Chit. Now we need to protect that seed, so we fence it with austerities, egolessness, and peacefulness. This fence prevents encroachers (bad society) and animals (ignorant people) from entering. Contentment and tolerance work as guards which are very alert to avert the enemies of expectation, attachment, lust, greed, pride, and so forth. When the seed, which is Sattva Guna, sprouts up, the weeds, which are Rajas and Tamas Gunas, grow with it. They try to cover up the tiny sprout, which is still very tender and small. Now again Asana, Pranayama, and meditation act as weeders; they cut back Rajas and Tamas Gunas, and the sprout of Sattva Guna starts to grow. It gives two leaves, the goal and the path. Both leaves are fed from the same stem — Sattva Guna, or wisdom.

Now this seed of concentration, which became a sprout, gets stronger and starts to branch. Truthfulness, contentment, egolessness, and compassion are the branches; and the plant becomes a tree which is strong enough to stand by itself. This tree is called Samadhi. When the tree, Samadhi, is mature it starts to flower with dispassion. When dispassion reaches perfection it loses itself and becomes the fruit, which is knowledge of God. One who has attained this fruit is freed from the three-fold desire — fame, wealth, and sensual pleasure — and the three-fold karma — past, present, and future — and attains the stage of supreme dispassion, Kaivalya.

That the world is untrue is Satyam (Truth)
To realize this truth is Jnanam (Knowledge)
Truth is the origin, Brahman (God)
Truth has no end, Anantam (Infinity)
All are the same. Yoga is for attaining this Truth.

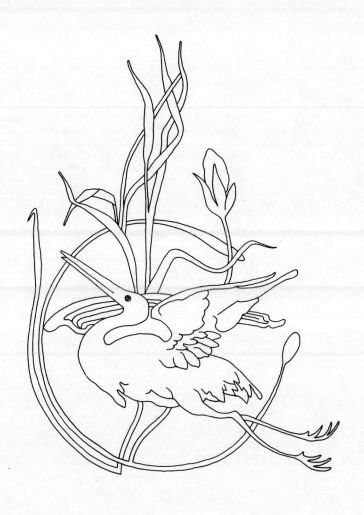

Each second of our lives is like a seed of grain, and time is a hungry bird eating every seed very quickly. When the grain is finished the bird will fly away. So worship God, surrender to Him, and attain peace.

GLOSSARY

Agami
Karma in the process of being created.

Aham Brahma
"I am God." A phrase of Self affirmation which is repeated as
a discipline of Yoga.

Ahamkara
Ego. The faculty of identification with the world; one of the
four minds.

Ahimsa
Non-violence; one of the five Niyamas.

Ajapa
A method of tuning mind and mantra with the breath.

Ajna
Order, command.

Ajna Chakra
Energy center located behind the eyebrows; the seat of one's own guru; the giver of orders.

Ajnana
"Without knowledge." A state of ignorance in which one identifies the world as real.

Anahata Chakra
Energy center in the spine located at the level of the heart; often called the Heart Chakra.

Anandamaya Kosha
"Bliss Sheath." A human being is composed of five sheaths, which are divided among three bodies: the Gross body consists of one sheath, Annamaya Kosha, the food sheath. The Subtle Body consists of three sheaths: Pranamaya Kosha, the breath sheath; Manomaya Kosha, the mind sheath; and Vijnanamaya Kosha, the intellect sheath. The Causal Body consists of the bliss sheath, Anandamaya Kosha, that which is closest to God.

Anantam
Infinity.

Aparigraha
Non-hoarding; one of the five Niyamas.

Asana
Postures; third limb of Ashtanga Yoga.

Ashram
Home, or living quarters, for a group of people with similar spiritual goals.

Ashru
Tears; one of Ashta Vikara, sattvic emotional changes.

Ashta Vikara
Eight purifying emotions: stiffness, trembling, sweating, change of color, weeping, cracking of voice, horripilation (gooseflesh, hair standing on end), fainting.

Ashtanga Yoga
"Eight-limbed Yoga." A comprehensive system of Yoga which combines disciplines for the body, breath, mind, and spirit.

Asteya
Non-stealing; one of the five Niyamas.

Atma Vichara
"Who Am I?" The practice of Self inquiry.

Aum, or Om
Primordial sound of God.

Avidya
A state of ignorance; the level with which sadhana begins.

Ayurveda
Classical Indian medical science.

Baivarna
Change of color; one of eight emotional changes.

Bhagavad Gita
Hindu scripture in which Krishna explains Karma Yoga, Bhakti Yoga, and Jnana Yoga.

Bhagavata Purana
Hindu scripture.

Bhakti Yoga
The path of devotion, worship.

Bhava Pratyaya
Born with extraordinary powers.

Bindu
Center point of chakras where energy is concentrated; seed; semen.

Brahma
God, as the creator.

Brahmachari
"One who walks on God's path." One who restrains sexual desire.

Brahmacharya
Continence; a sect that practices sexual restraint.

Buddha
A saint born about 568 B.C. in India on the border of Nepal in a kingly family; the founder of Buddhism.

Buddhi
Intellect; one of the four minds, having to do with the faculty of discrimination.

Chaitanya Mahaprabhu
A Bhakti Yoga saint who was born in 1407 and died in 1455.

Chakras
Foci of energy distributed along the spinal column and in the head.

Chit
Consciousness; memory. The highest of the four minds into which all the others must merge before liberation is possible.

Darshan
Spiritual audience.

Deva
Demi-god.

Dharana
Concentration;
sixth limb of Ashtanga Yoga.

Dhyana
Meditation;
seventh limb of Ashtanga Yoga.

Dvapar Yuga
Age of half-truth.

Ganja
Marijuana.

Ghee
Clarified butter.

Guna
Essential quality.
There are three Gunas of which everything
in the universe is composed:
Rajas Guna is creative, active, emotional energy;
Tamas Guna is resistant, inert, or destructive energy;
Sattva Guna is the energy of pure balance.

Guru
Teacher;
in Yoga, the spiritual teacher.

Guru Maharaj
Title of great respect for a spiritual teacher.

Hum Sah
"The great swan (the Self)." Mantra for Ajapa Pranayama, meaning "I am He."

Ishvara Pranidhana
Surrender of ego to God; fifth and final Niyama.

Jagrat
Normal waking state.

Japa
Repitition of God's name or Mantra.

Jiva
Individual being.

Jnana
Highest knowledge.

Jnana Shakti
Power of consciousness.

Jnanendriyas
Subtle senses; the "idea" of smelling, tasting, etc.

Kabir Dass
A great saint and poet who was born in 1455 and died in 1575.

Kali Yuga
Age of one quarter truth; our present time.

Kampa
Trembling; one of the eight emotional changes, Ashta Vikara.

Karma
The law of cause and effect; an action.

Karma Shakti
Power of matter.

Karma Yoga
Selfless action; all work is done for God.

Karmendriyas
Subtle organs of action: the consciousness of feet, hands, tongue, genitals, and anus.

Karmic
Anglicized adjective of Karma.

Khanda Pralaya
Partial rest.

Kirtan
Singing of spiritual songs.

Kosha
Sheath; a being is composed of five sheaths in three bodies (see Anandamaya Kosha).

Krishna
Incarnation of Vishnu (God, the preserver) in Dvapar Yuga.

Kriya Shakti
Power of action.

Kula Kundalini
"Body winding".

Kundalini
The energy by which a yogi transcends his body and the world; often called "serpent power".

Lahiri Mahshaya
A householder saint who died in 1895.

Laya Yoga
Disciplines for dissolving the mind.

Loka
Realm, or universe. Everything within our physical universe
is considered to be in Bhu Loka, or the lowest of seven realms.

Loka Lok
The highest of seven realms.

Mahabharata
Hindu scripture in which yogic life is explained in a story of
war between the Kauravas and the Pandavas, two kingly
families.

Maha Pralaya
The great rest between the cycles of Yugas.

Maha Yuga
"Great Cycle." A period comprising all four Yugas together,
or 4,320,000 years.

Manas
Mind; the recording faculty and the lowest of the four minds.

Mandala
A design that can be read as an instrument of energy.

Mantra
Syllable, word, or phrase that has power due to its sound
vibration.

Mastaka Granthi
"Head knot." One of three knots in the body that must be
broken through to achieve liberation; this, at the base of
the skull.

Mauna
Silence; a self-discipline.

Maya
God's manifestation as the world; hence, illusion.

Mudra
Special posture and/or visualization to intensify concentration.

Muladhara Chakra
Energy center at the base of the spine, where the latent power of Kundalini is stored until awakened.

Mula Prakriti
Source of all creation; the center of Sahasrara Chakra in the crown of the head.

Nada
Sound; in Yoga, subtle sound.

Nada Yoga
Discipline of concentrating on the subtle sound.

Nadi
Subtle nerve channel.

Nirdvandva
State of fearlessness.

Nivritti
Involution; the reverse of Pravritti; the stage when energy is drawn in and directed upward toward the realization of Self.

Niyama
Restraints; second limb of Ashtanga Yoga.

Ojas
Subtle electrical energy in the body.

Parama Siddha
One who has attained the highest knowledge.

Para Shakti
Combination of Jnana Shakti, Kriya Shakti, and Karma
Shakti in one; power of God.

Patala
Nether region.

Pingala, and Ida
Subtle nerves (Nadis) related to the breath flowing through
the right and left nostrils, respectively.

Pralaya
Fainting; one of the Ashta Vikara, emotional changes.

Prana
Vital force of life; breath.

Pranayama
Breath control; fourth limb of Ashtanga Yoga.

Pranic
Anglicized adjective of Prana.

Prarabdha
Fate; result of past karma already worked out.

Pratyahara
Mind control; fifth limb of Ashtanga Yoga.

Pravritti
Evolution; the stage where creative energy is flowing downward and spreading out; opposite of Nivritti.

Pulaka
Horripilation; gooseflesh, hair standing on end; one of Ashta Vikara, emotional changes.

Purusha
God as Self.

Raja
Subtle sexual energy in women; the equivalent of semen.

Rajas Guna
Creative energy; one of three essential qualities.

Rajasic
Anglicized adjective of Rajas Guna.

Rama
Incarnation of Vishnu, God as Preserver, in the Treta Yuga.

Ramakrishna Paramahansa
Great nineteenth century saint of Bengal, India.

Ramana Maharshi
Great saint who died in 1950.

Ramayana
Hindu scripture in which yogic life is explained in the story of Prince Rama.

Sadhana
Spiritual practices.

Sadhu
Renunciate; one who has taken religious vows.

Sahasrara Chakra
Thousand petal lotus in the crown of the head.

Samadhi
Superconsciousness; eighth limb and culmination of Ashtanga Yoga.

Samchit
Collected Karma, yet to be worked out.

Samskara
Impressions on the mind from past births.

Samta
Equality.

Samyama
A stage when Dharana, Dhyana, and Samadhi are perfected and used together.

Santosha
Contentment.

Satsanga
Sat, "truth"; sanga, "union"; gathering of people seeking the truth; reading scriptures.

Sattva Guna
The essential quality of pure balance.

Sattvic
Anglicized adjective of Sattva Guna.

Sat Guru
Spiritual teacher who is a Self realized being.

Satyam
Truth.

Sat Yuga
Age of truth.

Shabda
Sound.

Shakti
Power.

Shath Karma
Six purification practices for the inner and outer body.

Shiva
God as the destroyer, as the element of change and transformation.

Shunya
The void, beyond subject and object.

Skanda
A division of a major work in Sanskrit literature.

Siddha
One who has attained high powers.

Siddhis
Extraordinary powers, achieved in a high state of consciousness.

So Hum
Subtle level of the Hum Sah Mantra.

Sri Iso Upanishad
Hindu scripture.

Stambha
Stiffness, paralysis; one of the Ashta Vikara, emotional changes.

Sumeru
A mountain symbolizing the top of Shahasrara Chakra.

Sushumna
The main subtle nerve channel (Nadi), located in the spine.

Sushupti
Deep, dreamless sleep.

Svapna
Sleep with dreaming.

Svar Bhanga
Cracking of voice; one of the Ashta Vikara, emotional changes.

Sveda
Sweating; one of the Ashta Vikara, emotional changes.

Tamas Guna
Essential quality of inertia, resistance.

Tamasic
Anglicized adjective of Tamas Guna.

Tantra
System of Spiritual discipline that teaches through sublimation of emotions.

Tapas
Austerity; penance; self discipline.

Tattva
Element, of which there are five: Earth, Water, Fire, Air, and Ether.

Treta Yuga
Age when truth is three quarters predominant.

Turiya
Supernormal state; deep Samadhi.

Ujjayi Pranayama
Breathing technique in which the air is inhaled with a sobbing sound.

Vairag
State of dispassion.

Vikara
Change of form; defect; disorder.

Vijnana
Knowledge of the world; scientific understanding.

Vishnu
God as the preserver.

Vritti
Thought wave.

Vyana Prana
One of five Pranas; it spreads all over the body and four fingers' width outside the body, creating the aura.

Yama
Observances; first limb of Ashtanga Yoga.

Yantra
Instrument; a visual symbol composed of geometric forms.

Yuga
Cosmic age of creation.

PUBLISHER'S NOTE

When Baba Hari Dass is not teaching Yoga, or counseling
people, he is busy writing. He writes fables for children, stories
and plays for adults, treatises on Yoga, and philosophical
essays on the nature and meaning of existence. Sri Rama
Foundation is a nonprofit charitable corporation that was
established to publish Babaji's extensive writings. The profits
accrued by the Foundation will go to support destitute
children. A small orphanage has been established in India, and
we hope that other homes may be established in this country
in the future.

Other writings of Baba Hari Dass which have been published
by Sri Rama Foundation include HARIAKHAN BABA Known,
Unknown, a collection of stories and memories of one of
India's most advanced, yet little known, saints. THE MAGIC
GEM is a story-coloring book for children, the first to be
published of a series of fables by Babaji. Also, to be published
this Fall, is ASHTANGA YOGA, a complete exposition of
Babaji's specific teaching methods. It will complement
SILENCE SPEAKS as it presents in detail the different
practices of *sadhana*, which could be only touched upon
in this volume.